The Fiona Quilt Block

14 Projects from Sassy to Classy

Carolyn Perry Goins

Schiffer Publishing Ltd
4880 Lower Valley Road • Atglen, PA 19310

Other Schiffer Books on Related Subjects:
Heirloom Quilt Designs for Today, Lorie Martin & Jim Burnley, 978-0-7643-2669-1

Japanese Contemporary Quilts and Quilters: The Story of an American Import, Teresa Duryea Wong, 978-0-7643-4874-7

Quilts of Virginia, 1607–1899: The Birth of America Through the Eye of a Needle, Virginia Consortium of Quilters' Documentation Project, 978-0-7643-2465-9

Published by Schiffer Publishing, Ltd.
4880 Lower Valley Road
Atglen, PA 19310
Phone: (610) 593-1777; Fax: (610) 593-2002
E-mail: Info@schifferbooks.com

For our complete selection of fine books on this and related subjects, please visit our website at www.schifferbooks.com. You may also write for a free catalog.

This book may be purchased from the publisher. Please try your bookstore first.

We are always looking for people to write books on new and related subjects. If you have an idea for a book, please contact us at proposals@schifferbooks.com.

Schiffer Publishing's titles are available at special discounts for bulk purchases for sales promotions or premiums. Special editions, including personalized covers, corporate imprints, and excerpts can be created in large quantities for special needs. For more information, contact the publisher.

Library of Congress Control Number: 2015946623

Designed by RoS
Cover design by Brenda McCallum
Type set in Janda Elegant Handwriting/Alexon

ISBN: 978-0-7643-4981-2
Printed in China

Dedication

To my husband, who realized early in our marriage that fabric would be a rival in our relationship. Good man that he is, he has learned that if you can't beat them, join them. He now knows almost as much about quilting as I do. Also to my granddaughter, Fiona, for whom I have named the block.

Acknowledgments

I wish to thank the many people who have supported me in my vision of the Fiona block. First to my husband, whose encouragements and statements of "I'm so proud of you" kept me going forward. Thank you to my family for enduring many viewings of every quilt in various stages of completion. They always responded with, "May I have that quilt when it's finished?"

Thanks to my quilting buddy, Renelda Pedunas-Harter. We bounce ideas off each other and plan road trips, stopping at quilt shops along the way. Thanks also to:

The members of Waterford Quilt Guild who tested my pattern. They made helpful suggestions, and lovely quilts, too.

Wendy Web who proofread my manuscript.

Nancine Pike and Christy Dillon, talented long arm quilters. They have been wonderful with suggestions for quilting designs for the quilts. Nancine enjoyed the testing workshop so much she volunteered to make a quilt for the book.

Cindy Simms, who has been supportive with her knowledge of quilting in general.

The Mason-Dixon Quilt Professionals Network; members of this group share information and support to each other in the different venues of the industry.

Web Fabrics, where I worked for several years learning the business side of the industry and whose owner let me touch as much fabric as I wanted.

Laura Jaquinto, marketing director of Windham Fabrics, who took a chance and gave me my first national commercial opportunity.

Windham Fabrics, which has donated fabric to my project.

Hoffman Fabrics of California, which has donated fabric to my project.

Contents

Introduction

I have never had a problem choosing fabric. I love everything about it—the colors, themes, patterns, and prints. Just as other people might collect fine art, we quilters collect fabric, simply for the beauty of it. Fabric engages our senses and makes us feel good. I once met someone who actually decorated her home with bundles of fabric. Another person might buy two pieces of the same fabric, one to use on a quilt, and the other to look at.

Not many of us go to these extremes; we do want to use our fabric. When the stash begins to overflow, the obvious solution is to make a quilt. But what pattern or block will show off the fabric best? Do I have time to make pattern A or the skills to make pattern B?

The versatile Fiona block is the solution. Although it looks formal, the construction is simple. A quilter will be able to finish the project before losing interest, or, more likely, before another pressing project looms. The flexible Fiona block complements any theme, from Asian prints and batiks to scrappy fabrics. Setting variations—on-point, horizontal, with sashing, or with no sashing—will change the appearance enough that it will be unrecognizable as the same block.

This book includes instructions for five finished block sizes: 12″, 10″, 8″, 6″, and 4″. If you choose a different size, the construction will be the same; only the fabric requirements will change. Thimble symbols denote each project's level of difficulty. This may be the only quilt pattern you will ever need.

Fabrics and Tools

The question to ask before starting a quilt is what fabric to use. Do you wish to use a collection of designer fabric, or to deplete your stash? Is the quilt to be planned or scrappy, set on-point or horizontal, sashed or not sashed? Here are some hints to help create the perfect quilt.

An on-point setting will look best with a coordinating collection, or you can use a bridge factor to tie it together. The bridge may be a theme, such as in the *Full Bloom* quilt, or a single color or fabric appearing in each block. A formal look can be achieved by using the on-point style with sashing with or without the cornerstones, thus giving the quilt a more planned appearance.

Scrappy quilts are fun to make and great for using leftovers. Scrappy quilts are less formal; thus a horizontal look may be more pleasing to the eye and certainly easier to make. A theory on scrappy quilts is that the greater variety of fabric used, the better the quilt will look. However, a recurring color or fabric theme will give the quilt continuity.

Many quilters have a favorite color that dominates their scrap stash. A quilt of two color values (light and dark) or in two color families might be an option. Remember all the leftover bits from other projects? Perhaps using them to make a Fiona block wall hanging or baby quilt in the 6″ or 4″ block will use them up.

Several of the quilts shown in this book have an inner and outer border. The choice is yours. Always remember it is your quilt, and the options are design elements. If you like it, use it. There is no wrong choice.

Choosing Fabrics

Using manufacturer fabric collections is easy, as the designers have done all the hard coordinating work for you. But if you are putting your own scheme together, basic color theory applies. Don't panic—it is easier than it sounds. The rule is that color is divided into three values: light, medium, and dark. For example, the Fiona block may use a dark center strip. The side strips consist of two rectangles sewn together to equal the center block length. These may be medium or light colors. Remember that the side strips have a supporting role in this block.

Tip: Directional fabrics will not work well with the on-point layouts of the Fiona block.

Medium and light tones can have a range of intensity. The important thing is that a fabric looks good next to the one beside it. There are some wonderful books on quilting color theory. Lynne Roddy Brown's *Simple Strategies for Scrap Quilts* and Alex Anderson's *Let's Go Shopping for Fabrics* are among my favorites.

Amount of Fabric

I rarely buy less than one yard of fabric. If I really like it, I buy two or three yards. If I think it would make a good backing, then four yards works well for the quilt sizes I make. Novelties work well as the focus fabric for this block—a fat quarter would be enough for three center strips at maximum. If you want to use the same fabric for all of the center strips, you may need more yardage, depending on the number of blocks in the quilt.

Tools

Rotary cutting is helpful because it is quick and accurate. Safety is foremost. Remember that rotary cutters are rolling razor blades. Make securing the safety button a habit, a muscle memory. Be sure that the screw holding the blade is not too tight or too loose. The blade needs to roll easily.

> *Tip: Secure the safety button when completing each cut. Keep rotary cutters out of reach of children and pets.*

You will also need a rotary cutting mat. Wipe it clean of dust and fibers periodically. Keep mats out of the heat and direct sun to avoid warping.

Acrylic rulers. An acrylic ruler is a see-through ruler with readable measurement markings. They are made in every size and shape imaginable. A 6″ x 24″ ruler is a good start to a collection, followed by a ruler $6\frac{1}{2}$″ square. I also like having a $12\frac{1}{2}$″ square.

Thread

Threads come in every color and weight (thickness) one can imagine. For sewing machine piecing, I suggest using 50-weight thread. Many experienced quilters are now using 50-weight 2-ply threads, which are thinner. The effect is a flatter fold over the seams. Check the spool end label for information about the thread. I personally like Wonderfil™ or Aurifil™ threads for piecing.

To choose a thread color, lay out a few fabrics on the table and "puddle" a length of thread on them. Does the thread blend in with most of the fabric or stand out? Beige and tan threads work well with beige, yellow, pinks, orange/red—in other words, warm colors. Gray thread works well with cool colors such as dark red, blues, greens, and purples.

BSS

BSS stands for basic sewing supplies: thread, scissors, hand needles, straight pins, seam ripper, thimble, chalk marker, rubber disk, and lint brush for the sewing machine. I also add a pencil (mechanical and a #2), small ruler, and short bamboo skewer to my sewing kit.

Sewing machine. Keep your sewing machine clean of lint. A machine that is used often should be serviced every year. After all, you have your car tuned up to keep it in running order. Machines have gears that need to be serviced, cleaned, and oiled.

At home, clean the lint from the bobbin area each time you change the bobbin. A machine lint brush or cotton swab works well. I clean every area I can after finishing a project. Never use canned air to clean, as it will blow the lint deeper into the machine. A well-maintained machine can last decades.

Scissors. Large 8″ scissors should be used only for cutting fabric. I have two pairs clearly marked—one for fabric, one for paper. A small 3″ scissors is handy to have next to the sewing machine to cut threads.

Seam ripper. A sharp seam ripper is a necessity. It is a fact of life; we all have to remove a seam at some time. A sharp seam ripper will do the job quickly and without stretching the fabric. There are several styles available, and some have a built-in-light so you can see the thread better.

Straight pins. Long, thin pins with a flat head or yellow ball head work best for piecing. Short pins that are made for dressmaking can become lost in piecing. Appliqué pins are very short (1″) and are helpful in paper piecing.

Fabric marker. Markers come in a variety of types and colors. Some will disappear when rubbed or washed with cold water. Use whatever works best for you. Ask experienced quilters in your area what they prefer and why.

I use powdered chalk markers. A tube with a small disk in the end releases a line of chalk as it rolls along the fabric. It will rub off with a brush of the hand and not is affected by heat.

Rubber disk. A rubber disk can help pull a needle or pin through fabric.

Bamboo skewer. Bamboo skewers are useful for pushing fabric under the sewing machine foot, thus keeping fingers out of the danger area. Skewers also can be used as leverage to open or close quilter's safety pins when basting a quilt.

General Instructions

The Block

The Fiona block is easy to assemble. The block consists of two different-size rectangles: one long rectangle that acts as the center focus, and a smaller rectangle half the length of the center rectangle. Two of the smaller rectangles are sewn together to equal the length of the center piece and sewn on each side of it.

Diagram 1

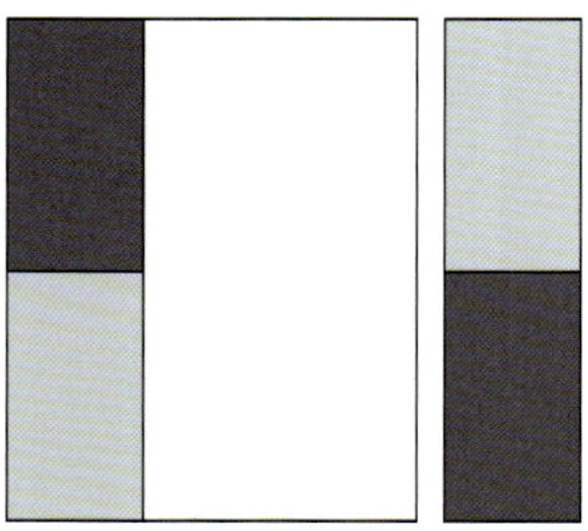

The center rectangle is wider than the side rectangles. This makes the block ideal for showcasing novelty fabrics. The cutting measurements for each size block are given in the chart below. All measurements include seam allowance. *(Diagram 1)*

FINISHED BLOCK SIZE	CENTER cut 1 at:	SIDES cut 4 at;
4″	2 1/2″x 4 1/2″	1 1/2″x 2 1/2″
6″	3″x 6 1/2″	2 1/4″x 3 1/2″
8″	4″x 8 1/2″	2 3/4″x 4 1/2″
10″	4 3/4″x 10 1/2″	3 3/8″x 5 1/2″
12″	5 1/2″x 12 1/2″	4″x 6 1/2″

Note: *All seam allowances are ¼" unless otherwise stated.* Consistent seam allowance will ensure accurate size of blocks and make it easier to assemble the quilt top.

Directions are given in rotary cutting format. Strips are cut to stated measurement and individual pieces are cut from the strips.

Seam intersections: These are also known as opposing seams. Two units, their seam allowance pressed in opposite directions, are placed with right sides of fabric together. The seams should butt up to each other, each seam acting as a wall to keep the other fabric from shifting. Place a straight pin perpendicular through the two layers on one side of the seam intersection. Place another pin on the opposite side of the seam intersection and stitch.

Piecing: Place two pieces of fabric with right sides together, pin at the edge to be sewn. Pins should be inserted perpendicular on the edge, meaning the pin is vertical to the horizontal edge of fabric. Place pinned unit under presser foot of sewing machine and sew a 1/4″ seam. *(Diagram 2)*

Diagram 2

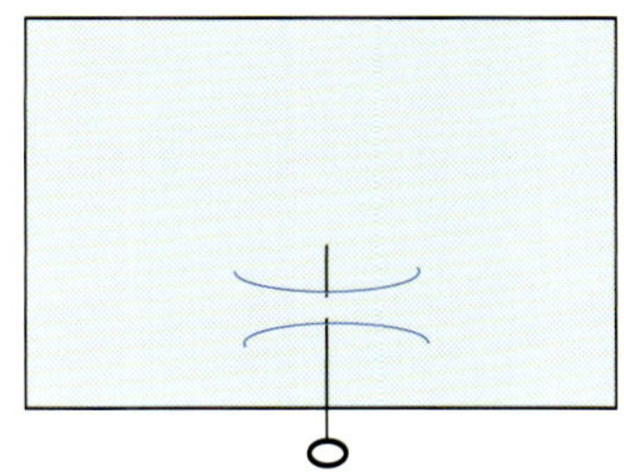

Chain piecing: I recommend this whenever possible, as it saves time and thread. Sew a seam, but do not stop and remove the unit from machine. Sew "in the air" for a few stitches and slide the next unit under the presser foot. The feed dog will catch the fabric and pull it under the foot to continue sewing. Keep going until all units are sewn. Cut the thread, leaving a 1/4″ tail and remove from machine. The connected units will resemble a kite tail. Clip threads to separate the units.

Pressing: Usually seam allowances are pressed to the darker fabric, and the same is true with the Fiona block. The adjoining side seams are pressed to the opposite sides, regardless of the color. This makes the seams less bulky. Be consistent. The side to center seams will press to the center. Sashing, cornerstones, and borders are pressed toward themselves.

Triangles, half squares, and quarter squares: The Fiona block will require side insets (triangles) when using an on-point/diagonal layout to create straight outer edges. The measurements and cutting directions are given in each pattern.

Diagram 3

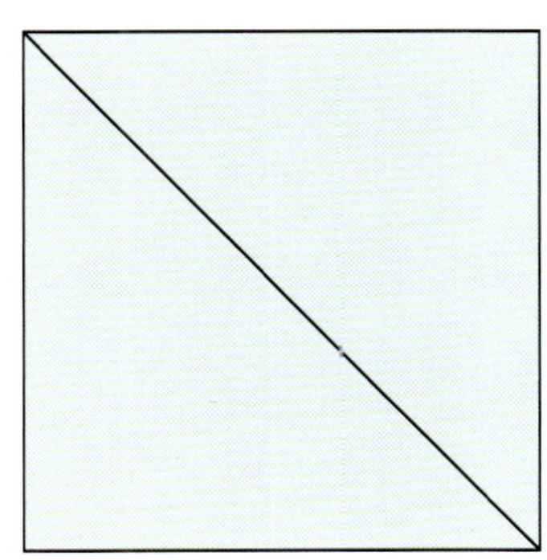

A half-square triangle is a square that is 7/8″ larger than the finished size. It is cut once on the diagonal. The straight of grain will be on the short sides of the triangle. *(Diagram 3)*

Diagram 4

Quarter-square triangles, or X cuts, as I call them, are often used for the side insets of an on-point layout. A square is cut at least 1 1/2" larger than the finished size. The square is then cut twice on the diagonal, thus the X cut. The result is four triangles with the straight of grain on the long edge. *(Diagram 4)*

Tip: If triangles are used as insets, it is okay to increase the square size ½" to 1" larger than the chart states. They can easily be trimmed later.

FINISHED BLOCK SIZE	CUT SQUARE FOR CORNER	CUT SQUARE FOR SIDE INSET
4"	3 3/4"	7"
6"	5 1/8"	9 3/4"
8"	6 5/8"	12 5/8"
10"	8"	15 1/2
12"	9 3/8"	18 1/4

Sashing and cornerstones: Sashing frames and separates the blocks and is used to increase the size of the quilt and/or accent the design. Sashing strips may be added regardless of whether the layout is horizontal or on-point. The strips can stand on their own or have cornerstones (small squares at the corners of each block). The sashing strips are cut the length of each block and sewn to one side of the block, and to both sides of the first and last block in the row. A long sashing strip is sewn to the top of each row of blocks, and then the next row of blocks is sewn to the strip. Mark the sashing strip where the block intersects the seams so the next row of blocks will align along the intersections.

Cornerstones are squares the same width as the sashing, usually in a contrasting fabric. They are sewn between each block of sashing along a row. *(Diagram 5)*

Diagram 5

On-point layout: This is not as difficult as it appears. If you tilt your head and view it at an angle, you will see the horizontal rows. The rows always contain an odd number of blocks. The upper and lower corners will be single blocks. The next row will have three blocks. The number of blocks will increase and then decrease according to the quilt size.

Insets for on-point: The block size will determine the size of the inset triangle. Refer to the chart for size. Insets are quarter-cut (X-fashion) triangles. Pin a short side of the triangle to the side of the block. The point of the triangle will extend beyond the block by 1/4" or more. The straight edge should be even with the bottom of the block. The long edge will be at an angle. A work surface or design wall will help to ensure accurate placement. *(Diagram 6)*

Diagram 6

Halfway through the quilt top, the angle will change to the opposite direction. *(Diagram 7)*

Diagram 7

Corners are half-square triangles. As a square quilt requires four corners, two squares of fabric are needed and each is cut once on the diagonal to create these four corners. *(Diagram 8)*

Diagram 8

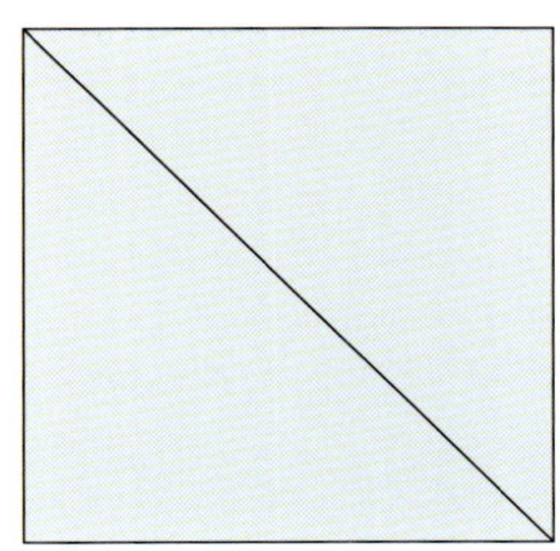

The long edge is bias, meaning it stretches easily. The use of several pins is recommended. This long edge will be pinned to the top edge of a corner block. The short sides of the triangles are straight of grain to ensure stability to the quilt top. *(Diagrams 9& 10)*

Diagram 9

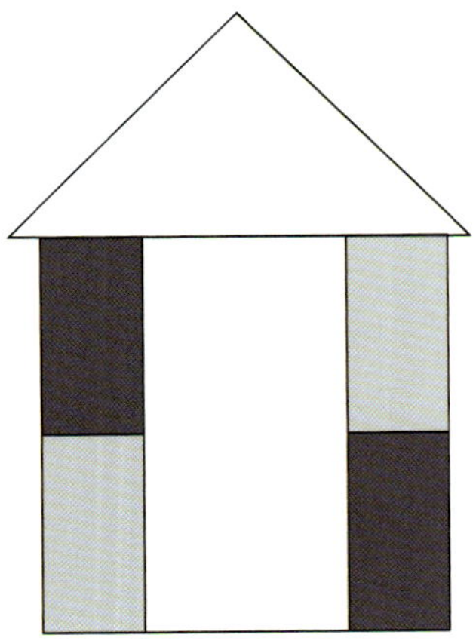

Diagram 10

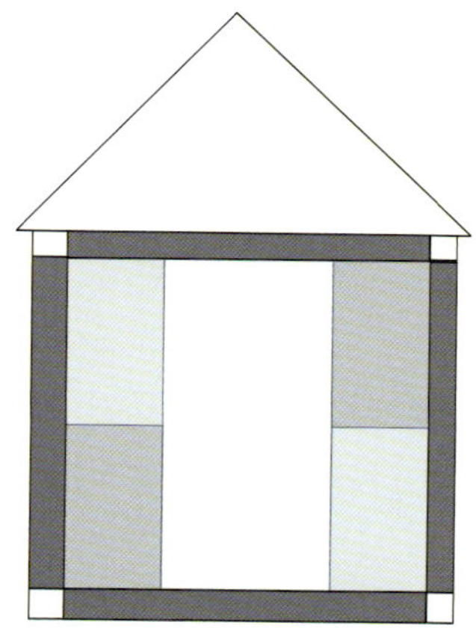

Corner triangle sewn to a plain block and a sashed block.

Diagram 11

Borders: If the border measurement is longer than the border fabric, you will have to join two strips. Place strip ends, right sides together (picture-frame style) and pin. Draw a $\frac{1}{4}$" seam line across the strip to the other end at a 45-degree angle. Sew on the line, and open to see if strip is straight. Trim away excess fabric, leaving a $\frac{1}{4}$" seam allowance. This procedure also may be used to join binding strips. *(Diagram 11)*

Diagram 12

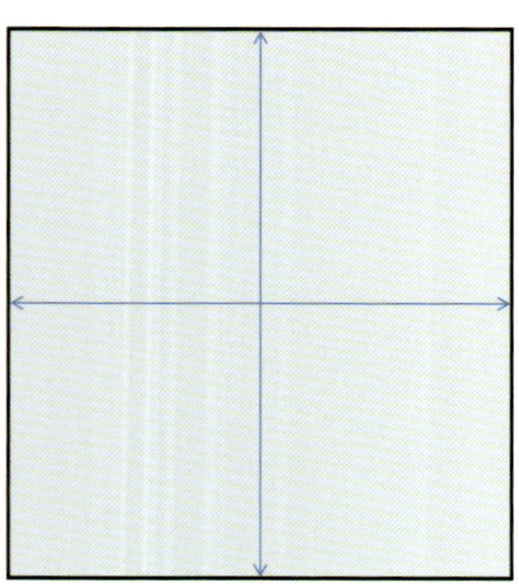

Measure quilt top for borders: The outside edges may have stretched. Place the quilt top on a flat surface and measure top to bottom and side to side through the middle. *(Diagram 12)*

Tip: Mark the quilt at middle and quarter points with a chalk marker. Mark the border strips at measurement points and use straight pins to align the border strips.

Binding: Directions are for a double-fold French binding. Fabric requirements for binding are based on $2\frac{1}{2}$″ strips. If you want a narrower binding and are comfortable sewing it, go for it. The strips are cut straight of grain (length or width of fabric). A bias binding is reserved for scallop or curved edges.

Diagram 13

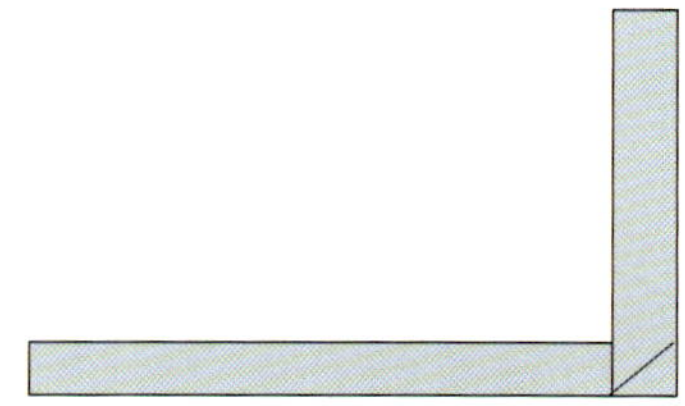

Formula for binding yardage: Measure all sides of the quilt. Add all the numbers and divide by 40, rounding up, to get the number of strips needed. Multiply the number of strips by the width of the binding strip.

Example: 40″ (side) + 40″ (side) + 50″ (top) + 50″ (bottom) = 180″.

180 divided by 40 (width of fabric) = $4\frac{1}{2}$. Round up to 5 strips needed.

5 strips needed x $2\frac{1}{2}$″ (width of strip) = $12\frac{1}{2}$″. Round up to 13″x 40″ to get the amount of fabric needed. Follow the border instructions for joining binding strips. *(Diagram 13)*

Diagram 14

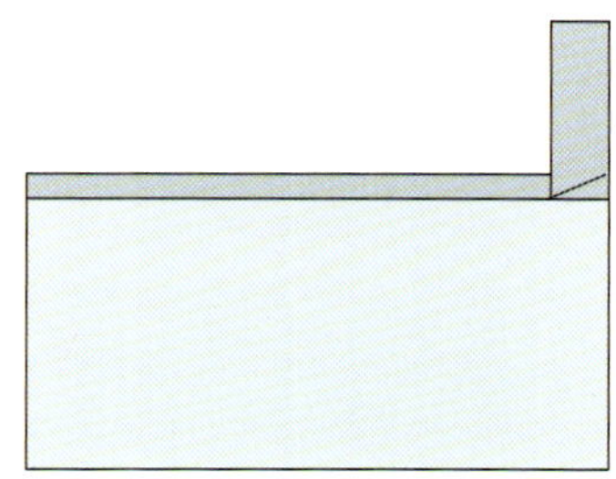

Join all strips together. Fold in half lengthwise and press into one long, narrow strip. Lay the binding on the quilt top, matching the binding raw edge and quilt top raw edge. Pin at the starting point. Lay binding around quilt top to make sure the binding seams do not fall at a corner. If they do, readjust the binding in either direction. Use a sewing machine to sew a $\frac{1}{4}$″ to $\frac{3}{8}$″ seam allowance. Starting 2″ from the beginning of the binding and stopping $\frac{1}{4}$″ from the first corner. Back stitch a few stitches, stop, and cut threads. Fold the binding up to create an angle fold; bring the bulk of the binding down again, stopping with a fold at the top of the quilt. Align with next side of quilt, but do not lose the folds. There should now be two even edges. Adjust raw edge of binding to raw edge of side of quilt top. There will be a total of three folds to be even; the first fold is upward, the second is even with the quilt top, and the third is even along the new side edge to be sewn. *(Diagrams 14 & 15)*

Diagram 15

Diagram 16

Place the machine needle about 1″ down from the new side corner and back stitch, stopping $\frac{1}{4}$″ from the top. The fold at the top should be free to move. Continue to sew along the edge to the next corner, stopping $\frac{1}{4}$″ from end. Repeat process around all edges until reaching the starting point. Fold the beginning edge of the binding back on itself so that there is no raw edge exposed. Sew the remaining binding, overlapping the starting point by about 1″. Trim away excess. Fold the binding to the back of the quilt and hand-stitch with matching thread. *(Diagram 16)*

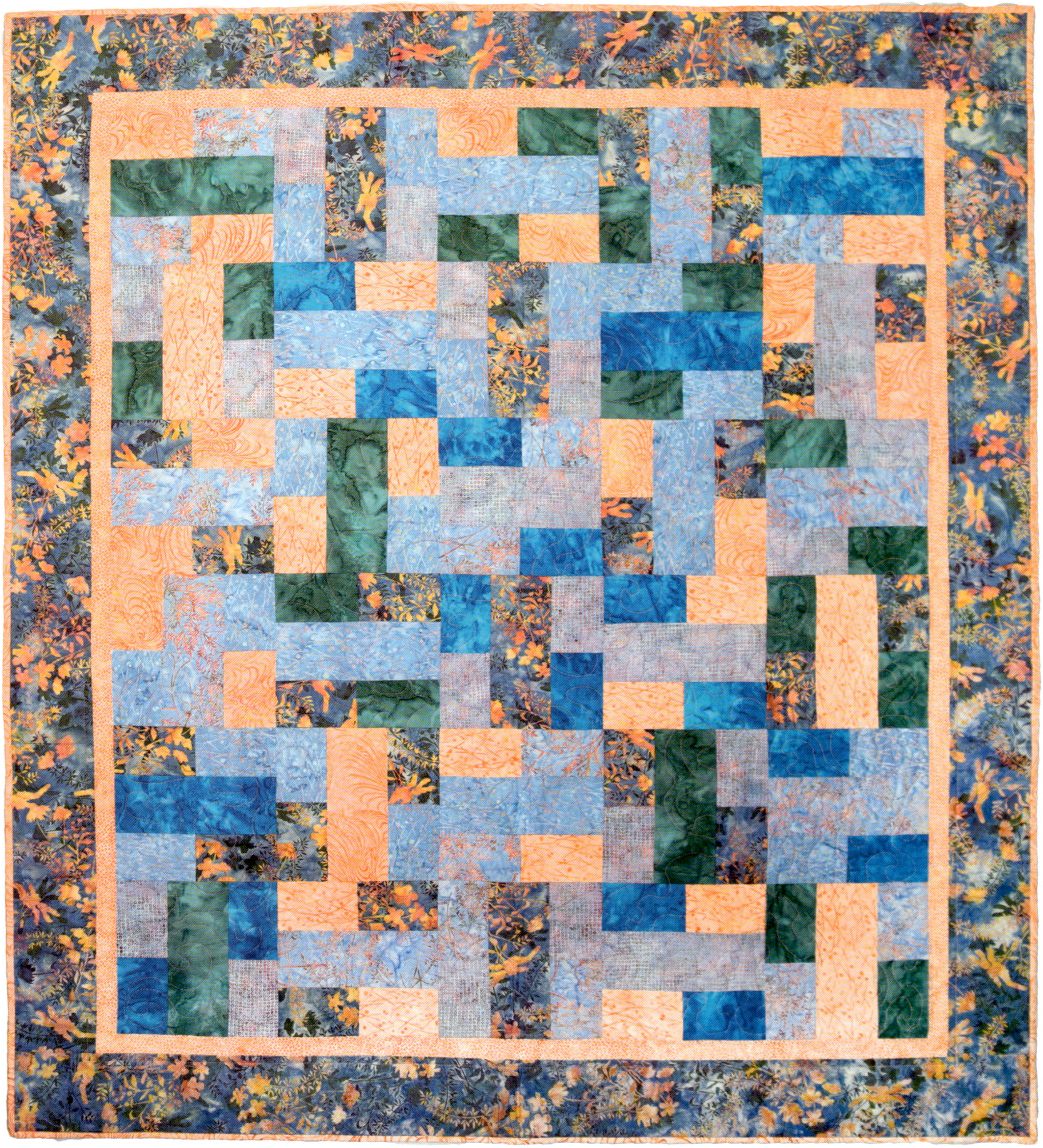

Coral Sea

1

Coral Sea

49"x 57", 8" finished block, 30 blocks

These bright colors make me think of the tropics. I have visions of glowing sunsets reflecting on tropical waters of blue, coral, and green. It is one of my favorite quilts. The size is suitable for a wall hanging or lap quilt. The blocks are set in alternating vertical and horizontal directions. I chose coordinating fabrics, but a scrappy look would be nice, too. My friend Renelda and I had great fun moving blocks until we found a pleasing layout. Thank you to Hoffman Fabrics of California for donating the batik fabrics.

Fabric:

$^1/_2$ yard each .... 7 coordinating fabrics
$^3/_4$ yard.............................. inner border and binding
$1^1/_4$ yard........................ .. blocks and outer border
3 yards........................... .. backing

Cutting: **center** 4″x 8½″, **sides** 2¾″x 4½″
Strips are cut the width of fabric. Because the outer border fabric will also be used in the blocks, cut the borders first and set aside. The remaining fabric may be used in the blocks.

Outer border: Cut 6 strips measuring 5″x 40″ and set aside. From the same fabric, cut 1 strip 4″x 40″. From this strip, cut 4 centers measuring 4″x 8½″.
Cut 2 strips 4½″x 40″. From this strip, cut sides measuring 2¾″x 4½″: 20 sides will be needed.

Centers and sides: From each fabric cut a strip measuring 4″x 40″. Cut from this strip 4 centers measuring 4″x 8½″. Cut 1 strip measuring 4½″x 40″ and cut side pieces measuring 2¾″x 4½″. Each strip yields 6 pairs of sides per color. If more sides of a particular color are required, then extra fabric is available.

Inner border: From the inner border fabric, cut 5 strips measuring 1½″x 40″ and set aside. The remainder may be used in the blocks.

Binding: From the binding fabric, cut 6 strips measuring 2½″x 40″ and set aside.

Block construction: Construct the blocks according to General Instructions (see page 10). Press seam allowances to the center strip. After cutting the pieces, lay them on a design wall or flat surface. The sides should have a pair of the same fabric within the block. The blocks are placed in alternating vertical and horizontal directions. *(Diagram 17)*

Diagram 17

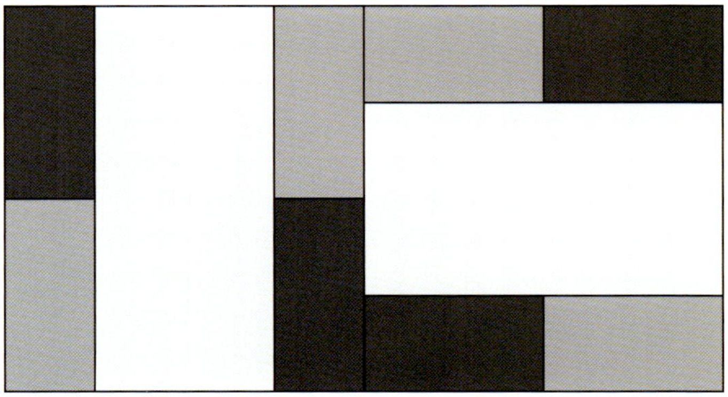

Sew together a row of 5 blocks and lay in the assigned place on the work surface. Continuing sewing blocks to create 6 rows. Press seam allowances in even-numbered rows to the right and in odd-numbered rows to the left.

Sew rows 1 and 2 together, aligning seam intersections. Sew row 3 to rows 1 and 2.

Sew rows 4 and 5 together, aligning seam intersections. Sew row 6 to this set.

Sew the two halves (rows 1, 2, 3, and 4, 5, 6) together aligning seam intersections. Press all row seam allowances to one direction.

Measure and square top, trim if necessary.

Measure quilt top for borders: See General Instructions.

Tip: Mark the quilt at middle and quarter points with a chalk marker. Mark the border strips at measurement points and use straight pins to align the border strips.

Inner border: Sew 2 strips together at the ends, creating an angle seam, as described in the General Instructions. Repeat process to create a total of 4 pairs. Pin and sew a paired strip to the side of the quilt. Trim excess even with quilt top. Repeat on all sides. Press seam allowance toward the border.

Outer border: Sew 2 strips together as above. Repeat the process to make 3 pairs. Sew one pair to the side of the quilt. Trim excess. Sew the other pair to the opposite side of the quilt. Trim excess. Sew a third strip to the top of the quilt. Trim excess. Pin excess strips together to create the last strip and sew it to the bottom of the quilt. Trim excess.

Baste the three layers — top, batting, and backing — and quilt as desired. The wide outer border will allow for an elaborate quilting design.

Binding: See General Instructions.

Texas Two-step

2
Texas Two-step

34"x 34", 8" finished block, 9 blocks

This red, white, and blue scrappy quilt will make a perfect baby quilt or wall hanging. It's small, easy, and takes very little fabric. made this quilt from leftovers of another project. It consists of nine blocks and an inner and outer border. A design wall or surface will help you arrange the pattern. Three blocks are alike in color and color placement; these blocks will be the "stepping stones." Think of the block placement as a tic tac toe game. Remaining color placements are random.

Fabric:

Scraps large enough to make two matching sides. I had extra of the border fabr c, so I use some of that fabric in the quilt body.

1/4 yard each .... 2 or 3 darks
1/4 yard each .... 3 or 4 mediums
1/4 yard each .... 4 lights
1/4 yard............................ light fabric for inner border
1/2 yard .... outer border
1/4 yard............................ binding
1 yard .... backing

Cutting: **center** 4″x 8½″, **sides** 2¾″x 4½″
Cut from border fabric 4 strips measuring 4¼″x 40″ and set aside. Any remaining fabric may be used in the quilt body.

Centers: Cut from dark fabrics 3 strips for centers measuring 4″x 8½″. Do not use the center fabrics for the "steps."

Inner border: Cut from inner border fabric 4 strips measuring 1½″x 40″ and set aside. Any remaining fabric may be used in the quilt body or the binding.

Binding: Cut from binding (if not using scraps) fabric 4 strips measuring 2½″x 40″ and set aside.

Diagram 18

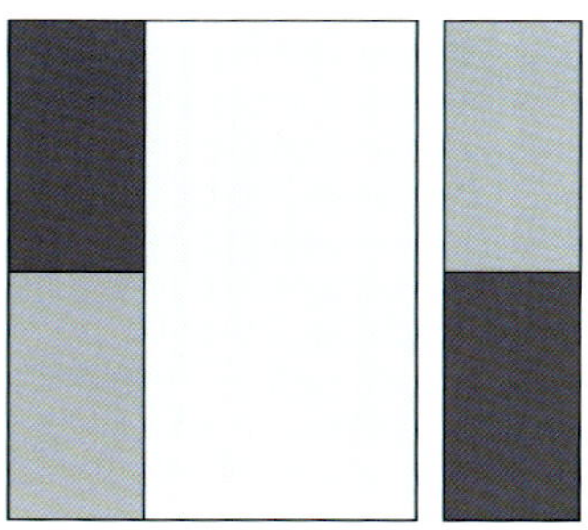

Block construction: Lay out the pattern on the design wall. Remember that while this is a random pattern, the sides should have a pair of the same fabric in diagonal placement within the block. Construct blocks according to General Instructions (see page 10). Press the side seam allowances to the center strip. *(Diagram 18)*

Place sewn blocks onto a work surface in alternating vertical and horizontal directions. When you are pleased with the arrangement, pin and sew blocks together, 3 blocks across and 3 down. *(Diagram 19)*

Diagram 19

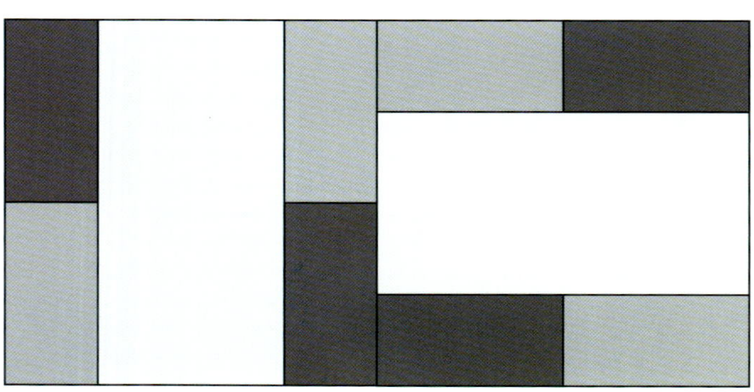

Measure quilt top for borders: See General Instructions.

> ***Tip:*** *Mark the quilt at middle and quarter points with a chalk marker. Mark the border strips at measurement points and use straight pins to align the border strips.*

Inner border: Pin one narrow strip to the side of the quilt top. Sew and trim even with quilt edge. Pin another strip to the opposite side of quilt. Sew and trim even with quilt. Pin third strip to top of quilt, sew and trim. Pin last strip to bottom, sew and trim.

Outer border: Repeat steps of the inner border. Baste the three layers — top, batting, and backing — and quilt as desired.

Binding: See General Instructions.

Cinnamon & Spice

3

Cinnamon & Spice

46"x 54", 8" finished block, 20 blocks

The quilt consists of 8″ blocks made with a classic but modern fabric. The side strips complement the colors of the focus fabric. Blocks are set horizontal, and the color placement creates a pinwheel effect. The corners have been trimmed in half-square triangles. The half triangle has a neutral background to create a curved effect. A wide border keeps the center pinwheels from rolling away.

Fabric:

1 1/2 yard .... focus fabric
7/8 yard .... each of 4 fabrics
1 fat quarter .... solid or muted background fabric
1/4 yard.................... inner border
1/3 yard .... binding
3 yards.................... backing

Cutting: center 4″x 8$^{1}/_{2}$″, sides 2$^{3}/_{4}$″x 4$^{1}/_{2}$″
The strips are cut to width of fabric. Four of the 20 blocks will be cut on the diagonal. The half blocks will be used as part of the corners.

Centers and sides: Cut from the focus color 4 strips the width of fabric measuring 4″x 44″. From each strip, cut center rectangles measuring 4″x 8$^{1}/_{2}$″. Each whole strip should yield 5 rectangles. A total of 20 are needed.
Cut from each of the 4 colors 3 strips measuring 2$^{3}/_{4}$″x 44″. From the strips, cut side rectangles measuring 2$^{3}/_{4}$″x 4$^{1}/_{2}$″. Each whole strip should yield 8 rectangles. You'll need 20 of each color.
Cut from the background fabric 4 squares measuring 8$^{1}/_{2}$″.

Inner border: Cut from inner border fabric 4 strips measuring 1$^{1}/_{2}$″x 44″ and set aside.

Outer border: Cut from the focus fabric for the outer border 5 strips measuring 6$^{1}/_{2}$″x 44″ and set aside. If a wider border is desired it may be cut, as long as there is enough fabric.

Binding: From binding fabric, cut 5 strips measuring 2$^{1}/_{2}$″x 40″.

Block construction: Follow the General Instructions (see page 10). Place fabric rectangles in 4 stacks according to fabric print. Pin and sew one rectangle to a different print rectangle to create a pair. Repeat with remaining prints to create consistent pairs. Continue to sew pairs using these two stacks. *(Diagram 20)*

Diagram 20

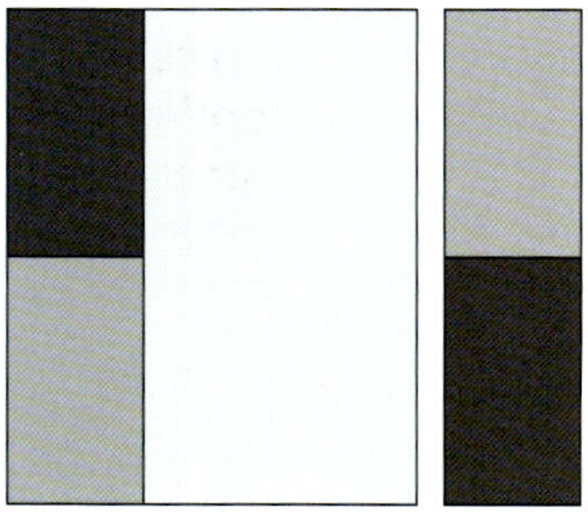

Arrangement of blocks: Place blocks on a work surface to play with placement. Remember that the sides should have a pair of the same light color value in diagonal placement within the block. The quilt has 4 blocks across and 5 down. The blocks are placed in an alternating direction so that the same colors meet in the middle of 4 connecting blocks. When layout is complete, remove one corner block at a time. Place a solid background square on top of the block, and pin to secure. Sew a diagonal seam from corner to corner, making sure the block is running in the correct direction. *(Diagram 21)*

Diagram 21

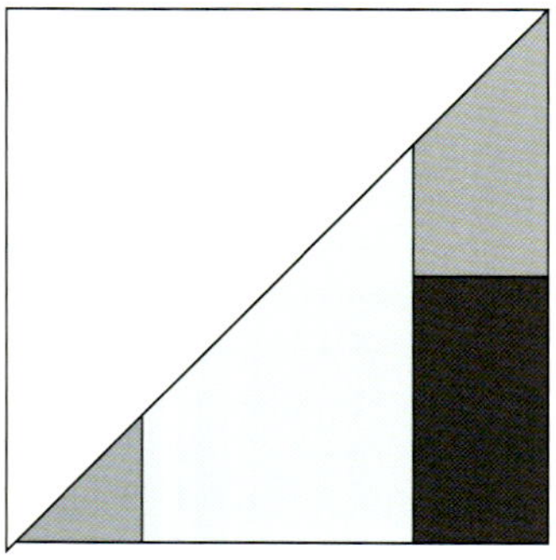

Example: Upper left corner block—sew top right to bottom left. Upper right corner block—sew top left to bottom right. Lower left corner block—sew top left diagonal to bottom right. Lower right corner block— sew top right to lower left. Trim, leaving a $^{1}/_{4}$″ seam allowance. Press seam allowance to background fabric.

Assembly: Place sewn corner blocks back into assigned place on work surface. Pin and sew blocks together to create rows of 4 across and 5 down. Press seam allowances in even-numbered rows to the right, and in odd-numbered rows to the left.

Sewing rows together: Pin row 1 to row 2, matching the intersection seams. Sew along seam line. Pin row 3 to row 4, matching the intersection seams. Sew along seam line. Pin row 5 to rows 3 and 4, matching the intersection seams. Pin the two sections (rows 1 and 2 to rows 3, 4, and 5), matching the intersection seams. Sew along seam line. Press seams in one direction.

Measure quilt top for borders: See General Instructions.

Tip: Mark the quilt at middle and quarter points with a chalk marker. Mark the border strips at measurement points and use straight pins to align the border strips.

Inner border: Pin one strip of inner border fabric to a side of pressed quilt top and sew a 1/4" seam allowance. Trim excess even with quilt top. Pin a strip to the opposite side of quilt and sew seam. Trim excess. Repeat on the top and bottom. Lightly press seam allowance to the border strip.

Outer border: Pin one outer border fabric strip to the side of the quilt top and sew. Trim even with edge of quilt top. Pin an outer border strip to the opposite side of the quilt top and sew. Trim excess fabric. Join two borders strips using method shown in General Instructions to gain length needed for top and bottom. Pin the joined border to the quilt top and sew. Trim excess fabric. Sew the leftover border strip to the last remaining full strip to gain the length needed. Pin to the bottom of the quilt top, sew, and trim. Press seams to inner border.

Tip: If the border fabric is shorter than the quilt top, you may need to join two strips. Place strip ends, right sides together (picture-frame style) and pin. Draw a 1/4" line across the strip to the other end at a 45-degree angle. Sew on the line, open to see if the strip is straight, and trim away excess fabric, leaving a 1/4" seam allowance. This procedure also may be used to join binding strips.

Baste the three layers — top, batting, and backing — and quilt as desired. I chose to highlight the circles of the fabric with my quilting.

Binding: Join binding strips and sew on edges as described in General Instructions.

Caribbean

4 Caribbean

65"x 77", 12" finished block, 20 blocks

This easy-to-make quilt is similar to Coral Sea in style and construction. Although it has a tropical feel, the muted colors are serene. A coordinated fabric collection, batiks, or traditional cloth will work, as it qualifies as a scrappy quilt. The blocks are set in alternating vertical and horizontal directions, and a wide border increases its total size. The block size makes this quilt ideal for a large bed—just increase the number of blocks. Thank you to Hoffman Fabrics of California for donating the batiks.

Fabric:

- 1/3 yard each .... 7 or more fabrics
- 1/2 yard .... inner border
- 2 1/4 yards .... outer border
- 1/2 yard .... binding
- 4 yards.............................. backing

Cutting: center $5^1/_2$"x $12^1/_2$", sides 4"x $6^1/_2$"

Strips are cut width of fabric. Because the outer border fabric will be used in the blocks, it is wise to cut the borders first and set aside. The remaining fabric may be used in the blocks. You'll need 20 centers and 80 sides.

Centers and sides: Cut from each coordinating fabric 1 strip for centers measuring $5^1/_2$"x 40". From this strip, cut 3 centers measuring $5^1/_2$"x $12^1/_2$". Also cut from all coordinating fabrics 2 strips measuring 4"x 40". Cut from each strip 6 sides measuring 4"x $6^1/_2$". Extra fabric is available if more sides of a particular color are needed.

Inner border: From the inner board fabric, cut 6 strips measuring $1^1/_2$"x 40" and set aside.

Outer border: From outer border fabric, cut 8 strips measuring 8"x 40" and set aside. Cut 1 strip $5^1/_2$"x 40". From this strip, cut 3 centers measuring $5^1/_2$"x $12^1/_2$". Cut 1 strip 4"x 40", and cut from this strip sides measuring 4"x $6^1/_2$".

Binding: From the binding fabric, cut 8 strips measuring $2^1/_2$"x 40" and set aside.

Block construction: Follow the General Instructions (see page 10) and press seam allowances toward the center strip. *(Diagram 22)*

Diagram 22

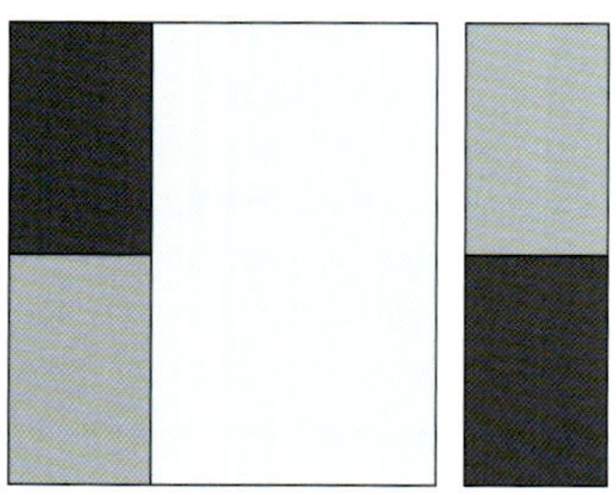

Assembly: Place the sewn blocks on a work surface in alternating vertical and horizontal directions. When you are pleased with the arrangement, pin and sew the blocks together to create rows of 4 blocks across and 5 down. Press the even number row seam allowances to the right. Press the odd number seam allowances to the left. *(Diagram 23)*

Diagram 23

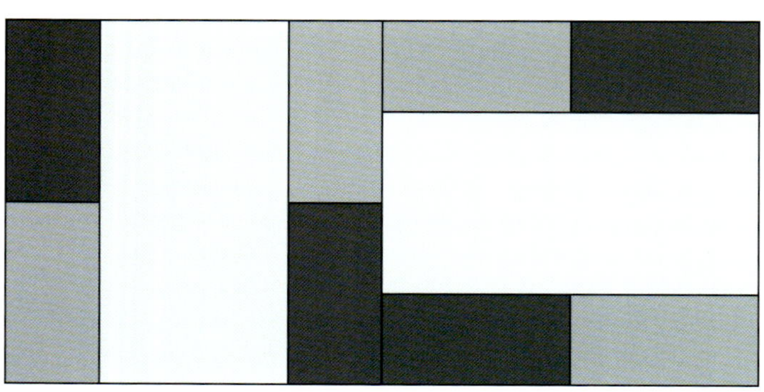

Sew rows 1 and 2 together, matching the seam intersections. Sew row 3 to rows 1 and 2. Sew rows 4 and 5 together, matching the seam intersections. Pin and sew the two sewn sections together (rows 1, 2, 3 to rows 4 and 5), matching seams. Press seam allowances in one direction. Measure and square top, and trim if necessary.

Measure quilt top for borders: Place the quilt top on a flat surface to measure from top to bottom through the center. Measure from side to side through the center, making sure to include the inner and outer borders.

Tip: Mark the quilt at middle and quarter points with a chalk marker. Mark the border strips at measurement points and use straight pins to align the border strips.

Inner border: See the binding section under General Instructions. Pin and sew 2 strips together, creating an angled seam. Pin and sew a paired strip to one side of quilt, and trim excess. Pin and sew the second pair of strips to opposite side, and trim excess. Cut the end of the excess strips straight and sew to the remaining whole strips. Pin and sew the third strip to the top of the quilt. Pin and sew the remaining strip to the bottom of the quilt. Trim excess.

Outer border: Sew 2 strips together, following the binding directions. Repeat process to make a second pair. Sew one pair to each side of the side quilt and trim excess. Repeat for top and bottom borders. Baste the three layers—top, batting, and backing—and quilt as desired.

Binding: See General Instructions.

Woven Rust

5 Woven Rust

34"x 34", 6" finished block, 31 blocks

This table topper will impress your guests as much as the food you serve on it. The pattern also makes a nice wall hanging or baby quilt. Imagine the seasonal color possibilities. The quilt consists of 6" blocks made from two color families. The side strips are the background, in this case black; several prints of the same value were used. Blocks are set on-point to accentuate the woven effect. The inset edges are completed blocks cut in half. The background colors are used in the binding. Do not let diagonal layout frighten you. As you complete the first row, you will see the directional process clearly.

Fabric:

$^1/_2$ yard .... color for center strip (focus fabric) ... 31 center strips are needed
1 fat quarter each.... 4 fabrics of dark color family .... 31 side strips each color needed
$^1/_3$ yard .... color of choice for binding
1 yard .... choice for backing

Cutting: center 3″x 6½″, **sides** 2¼″x 3½″
The strips are cut width of fabric. The quilt requires 25 whole blocks plus 6 blocks that will be cut in half on the diagonal. The half-blocks will be used as side insets. The corners will be left angular as a design element.

Centers and sides: Cut from the focus fabric 6 strips width of fabric measuring 3″x 40″. Cut rectangles measuring 3″x 6½″ from each strip. Each whole strip should yield 6 rectangles.
Cut from each dark fat quarter 4 strips measuring 3½″x 20″. From these strips, cut rectangles measuring 2¼″x 3½″. Each whole strip should yield 8 rectangles.

Binding. Cut from binding fabric 4 strips measuring 2½″x 40″.

Block construction: Follow the General Instructions (see page 10) . Details for this quilt are as follows: Place each side fabric rectangle in 4 stacks according to fabric print. Pin and sew one rectangle to a different print rectangle, creating a pair. Continue to sew pairs.

Tip: The side rectangles may be placed in a random or uniform pattern.

Diagram 24

Press seam allowance to either side. Place a side strip next to the center strip with right sides touching. Pin and sew along the length. Repeat with the second pair on the opposite side. Press seam allowances to the center. The block is now complete. Continue this process to complete all 31 blocks. *(Diagram 24)*

Arrangement of blocks: The blocks are set on-point (diagonal). The center strip should point right in the even number rows and left in the odd rows. This will create the woven effect. Refer to the picture.

Row 1 will have 4 blocks across with side points touching.

Row 2 will have 3 blocks set below row 1.

Row 3 will have 4 blocks across, a repeat of the first row.

Row 4 will have 3 blocks across.

Row 5 will have 4 blocks across.

Row 6 will have 3 blocks across.

Row 7 will have 4 blocks across. The seven rows will contain 25 blocks.

These outside edges will be filled with the remaining 6 blocks. Cut each remaining block on the diagonal, in the same direction, to create a triangle. Place the triangles along the edge of your design. The corners will not be filled.

Assembly: Pin and sew on the diagonal, placing the dog ear of the triangle at the top.

Row 1: Pin and sew the triangle to the block at the upper left corner and sew. Pin and sew the triangle on the opposite side of the block. *(Diagram 25)*

Diagram 25

Tip: This row should be straight along the bottom. After row 5 the triangle will turn 90 degrees and the dog ears will be at the bottom. The triangles will have a bias edge, so handle carefully. It is important to match the seam intersections when joining rows.

Row 2: This row has 3 blocks. Sew a triangle to the left side of the first block. Sew the block to the next block, and then to the third block. Sew a triangle to the right side of the third block, with straight edges along bottom of row. *(Diagram 26)*

Diagram 26

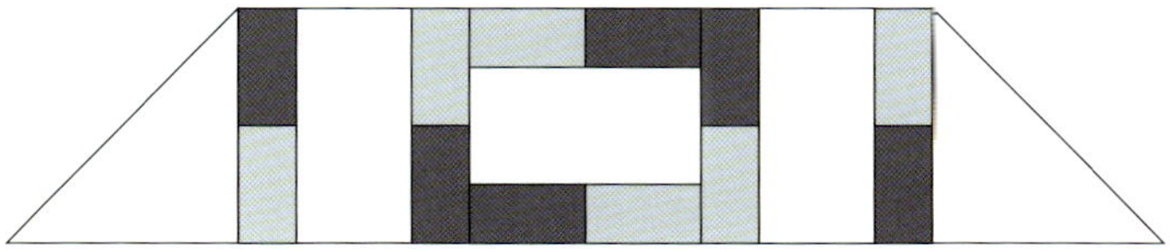

Row 3: Sew a triangle to the left side of a block. Pin and sew block to the next block. This row has 5 whole blocks. Pin and sew a triangle to the right side of the fifth block.

Row 4: No triangles will be sewn to this row. Pin and sew 5 blocks together.

Diagram 27

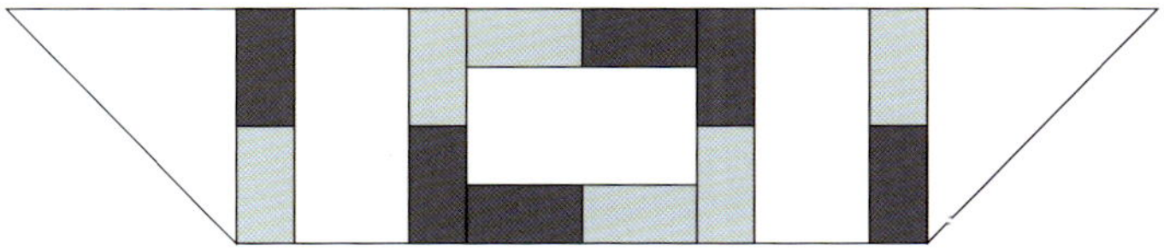

Row 5: The triangles will now be placed with straight edges along the top of the row. Sew a triangle to the left side of a block. Sew the block to the next block. This row has 5 blocks. Sew a triangle to the right side of the fifth block. *(Diagram 27)*

Row 6: Sew a triangle to the left side of a block. Sew block to the next block. This row has 3 whole blocks. Sew a triangle to the right side of the third block.

Row 7: Sew a triangle to the left side of the block. Pin and sew the last triangle to the last whole block. All the rows are complete and should have straight edges.

Press seam allowances to the right on the even-numbered rows. Press odd row seam allowances to the left.

Sewing rows together:

Pin row 1 to row 2, aligning seams. Sew along seam line.

Pin row 3 to row 4, aligning seams. Sew along seam line.

Pin rows 1 and 2 to rows 3 and 4, aligning seams. Sew along seam line to complete one-half of the quilt top.

Pin row 5 to row 6, aligning seams. Sew along seam line.

Pin row 7 to rows 5 and 6, aligning seams. Sew along seam line.

Pin the two halves, aligning seams. Sew along seam line. Press seams allowances in one direction. Top is complete. Due to the triangles being half-blocks, points will need to be trimmed.

Baste the top, batting, and backing. Quilt as desired. This piece was machine-quilted in a meandering pattern on a domestic sewing machine.

Tip: Closely baste the edges of the 3 layers to keep the bias edge from stretching.

Binding: Join binding strips and sew on edges as described in General Instructions.

6
Building Blocks

22"x 34", 6" finished block, on-point, 7 blocks

This item may be used as a wall hanging or table topper. The simple but modern design focuses on the fabric collection. The center panel—typically the focus fabric—is now used as background. Heavy quilting will make the fabric recede further so that the colorful side "bricks" pop out. This is an opportunity to show off your quilting.

This particular top was pieced in an afternoon. Deciding on the quilting design will take longer than piecing the quilt top. The rows are set on-point and require insets on the sides. This small quilt project is ideal for learning how to do on-point layouts.

Fabric:

1 yard .... background
$^{1}/_{2}$ yard red .... for inner border and binding
$^{1}/_{4}$ yard or fat quarter each of..... red, blue, purple, and green fabrics
$^{2}/_{3}$ yard .... backing fabric

Building Blocks

Cutting: **center** 3″x 6½″, **sides** 2¼″x 3½″

Centers, sides, and insets: Strips are cut width of fabric. Start with the color fabric for the sides first. Cut one strip measuring 2¼″x 40″. From the strip, cut seven rectangles of each color measuring 2¼″x 3½″. Set aside.

From the background fabric, cut seven rectangles measuring 3″x 6½″. This is the center of the block. Cut 2 squares measuring 9″ square. Cut the squares once on the diagonal, creating 4 half-square triangles for the corners. Set aside. Cut 1 square measuring 9¾″ on base and cut in X-fashion. There will be 2 extra triangles. These are the side insets. Set aside.

Inner border. From the red fabric, cut 3 strips measuring 1¼″x 40″. Set aside.

Binding. Cut 4 strips measuring 2¼″x 40″ for binding. Set aside. *(Diagram 28)*

Diagram 28

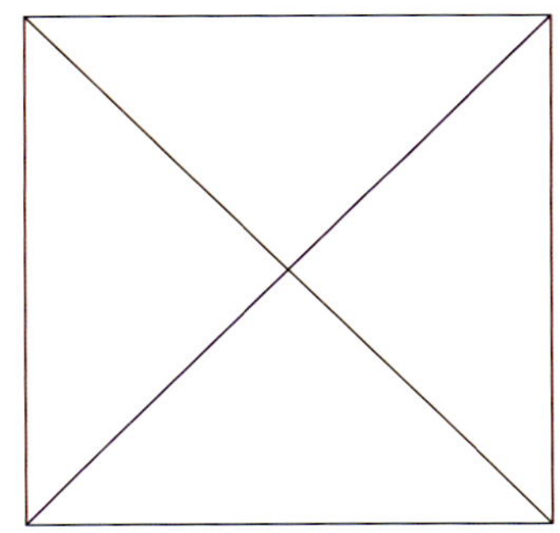

Outer border. Cut 4 strips from background fabric measuring 3½″x 40″ for outer border. Set aside.

Block construction: See General Instructions (see page 10). *(Diagram 29)*

Diagram 29

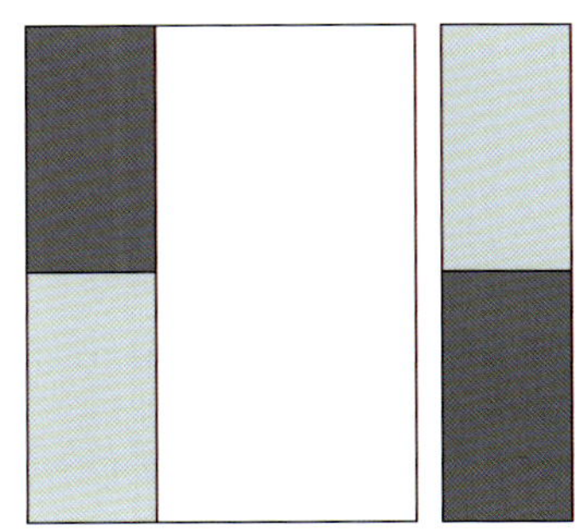

Details are as follows: Each color rectangle will be in same position within the block. Sew two colors together to create a pair. Repeat process until a stack of pairs is completed.

> *Tip: Chain piecing at this point helps to assure that the color placement is consistent. It also will save time and thread.*

Sew a pair of rectangles to each side of the center with right sides touching. Press the seams to the color sides.

Assembly: Sew 3 blocks end to end, making sure the colors are "marching" in unison, creating one long strip of background (center row). Sew another 2 blocks in same manner. Sew 2 more blocks in same manner, making sure all blocks are aligned in the same direction. *(Diagram 30)*

Diagram 30

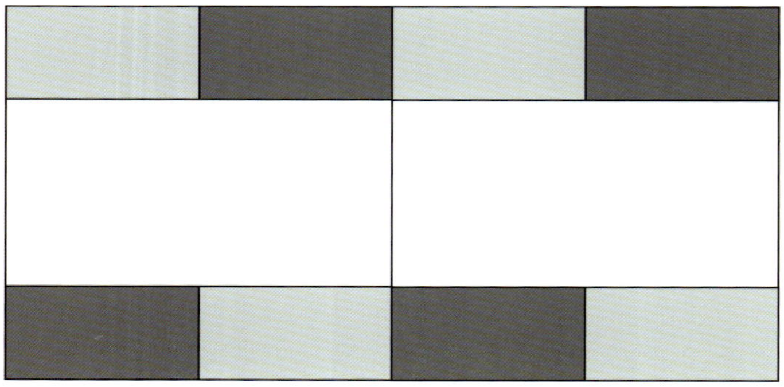

Place block rows on work surface. Row 1: Place a corner triangle on the side of the 4-block row (upper right corner) Pin and sew. *(Diagram 31)*

Diagram 31

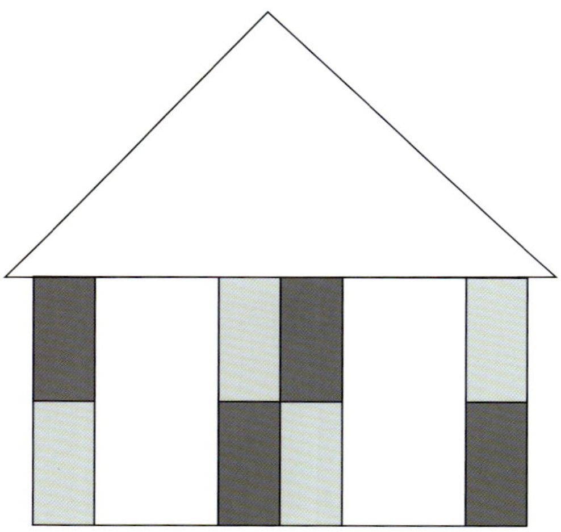

Place another corner triangle on the right side of the 4-block unit. *(Diagram 32)*

Diagram 32

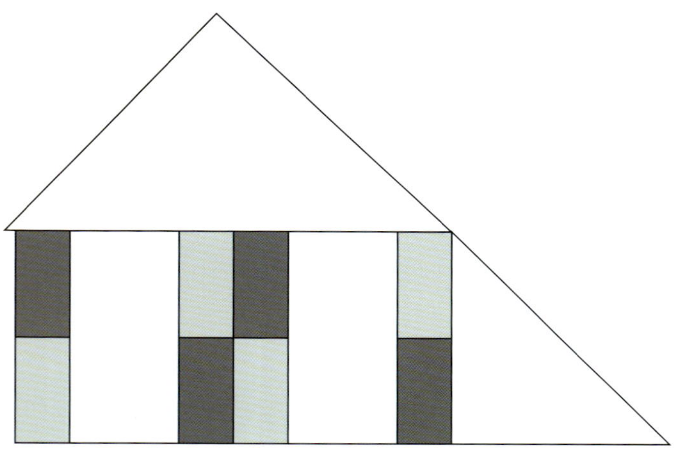

Sew an inset triangle to the lower right side of the first row. Place on work surface to match the color blocks. Refer to photo. Sew a corner triangle (half-square triangle) on the upper left corner unit (2 blocks). Check pattern on a work surface. Pin an inset triangle to the left upper end and sew. Sew the two units together, matching seam intersections. Pin the remaining corner to the last corner. Press seams toward the colors whenever possible. *(Diagram 33)*

Diagram 33

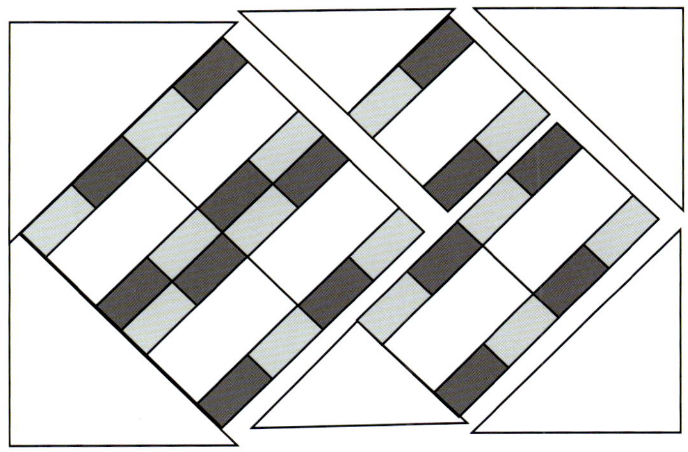

Measure quilt top for borders: See General Instructions.

Tip: Mark the quilt at middle and quarter points with a chalk marker. Mark the border strips at measurement points and use straight pins to align the border strips.

Inner border: Pin one strip to a side and sew. Trim excess. Sew another strip to opposite side and trim. Cut the last strip in half and sew one strip to the top of quilt. Sew the remaining strip to the quilt bottom and trim. Press seam allowance toward border.

Outer border: Sew one strip of background fabric to each side of the quilt and trim. Repeat on top and bottom edges of quilt. Press seam allowance to inner border. Baste the three layers and quilt as desired. I machine-quilted the negative spaces for a modern effect.

Binding: See General Instructions.

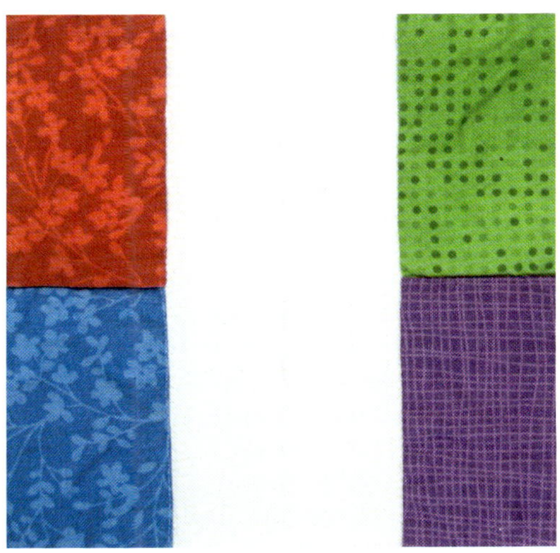

Red Poppies

7

Red Poppies

40"x 40", 8" finished block, 25 blocks

The unusual layout of these blocks gives the quilt a modern look. I remember seeing a painting similar to this in the home of a childhood friend in the 1960s. The pattern also resembles a maze. The monochromic color recedes into the background, while the bright red poppies seem to jump off the fabric. A heavy meander quilting reinforces the effect.

Fabric:

If you are using a directional focus print, purchase twice the amount of fabric.

7/8 yard .... bright large floral print
1/3 yard each .... small print, 4 or more same color and value
1/3 yard .... binding, should be contrast or same as bright color in print
1/8 yard optional .... contrast color to insert flat piping between quilt top and binding
1 1/2 yard .... backing

Cutting: **center** 4″x 8½″, **sides** 2¾″x 4½″, 25 blocks

Centers and sides: From the large floral print fabric, cut 5 strips to width of fabric measuring 8½″x 40″. From each strip, cut 8 center rectangles measuring 4″x 8½″.
From each of the four small print fabrics, cut 4 strips to width of fabric, 2¾″x 40″. Then cut 25 side rectangles measuring 2¾″x 4½″.

Binding: From the binding fabric, cut 4 strips measuring 2½″x 40″. Set aside.

Optional flat piping: Cut 4 strips measuring 1″x 40″. Fold in half (½″x 40″) and press flat. Set aside.

Diagram 34

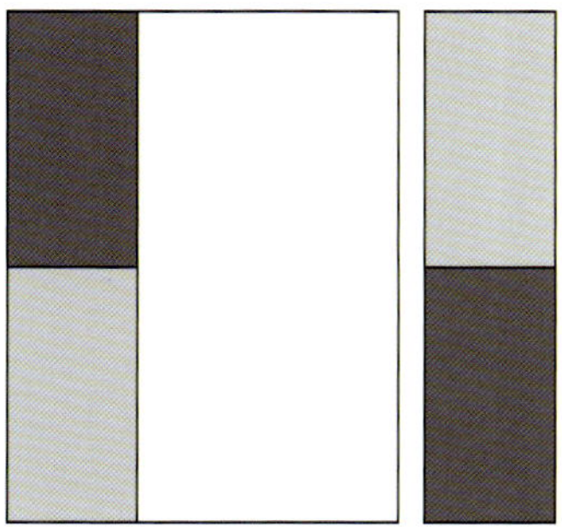

Block construction: See General Instructions (see page 10). The side fabrics are placed in the same position in each of the 25 blocks. Press seam allowances toward center. *(Diagram 34)*

Assembly: Place blocks on a work surface with the center lengthwise in the following order. There will be 5 blocks across and 5 blocks down.

Row 1: horizontal, horizontal, vertical, horizontal, horizontal

Row 2: vertical, vertical, vertical, vertical, vertical

Row 3: vertical, horizontal, horizontal, horizontal, vertical

Row 4: vertical, vertical, vertical, vertical, vertical

Row 5: horizontal, horizontal, vertical, horizontal, horizontal

Sew blocks in each row together. Return completed rows to the work surface. Continue to pin and sew block rows. Press seam allowances of even-number rows to the right and odd-number rows to the left.

Connect rows: Sew rows 1 and 2 together, matching seam intersections.

Sew rows 3 and 4 together, matching seam intersections.

Sew row 5 to rows 4 and 5, matching seam intersections.

Pin and sew the row 1 and 2 section to the row 3, 4, and 5 section to complete the top. Press seam allowances in one direction.

Baste the quilt, batting, and backing. Quilt as desired. Red Poppies has outline quilting around the flowers and heavy meandering in the background to accentuate the flowers. Trim and square quilt top.

Optional flat piping: Pin a single folded strip along the outer edge of quilted top, raw edge to raw edge. Baste with a 1/4″ seam the entire length of piping, and trim. Pin a strip to the next side (may pin opposite side or in clockwise direction) in same manner and sew. Repeat on all 4 sides.

Binding: Place binding on top of piping and follow the binding procedure in General Instructions. When binding is brought to back of quilt for sewing, the 1/4″ piping will be exposed.

Tea Time

8

Tea Time

52"x 52", 10" finished block, 16 blocks

Tea Time is an elegant, yet playful design. Think of the possibilities with children's prints. Only five fabrics are required for this novel look. Each fabric is placed in the same position on each block. The secondary design is created by twisting the direction of the block in the layout. The double border is unusual, as the inner border is wider than the outer border and completes the look. The 52″ square is ideal for a table topper, but if a small block size were used (8″) it would make a perfect baby quilt of 44″x 44″.

Fabric: *(Directional fabrics are not recommend.)*

1 yard .... focus theme fabric
1 yard .... light background, small print
1/3 yard .... light background, medium print
1/3 yard .... 2 dark fabrics
1/2 yard .... choice for binding
3 1/4 yard .... backing

Cutting: center $4^{3}/_{4}$″x $10^{1}/_{2}$″, sides $3^{3}/_{8}$″x $5^{1}/_{2}$″

Sides will be in the same placement throughout the quilt, so a strip cutting method may be used. Note tips on cutting sides.

Centers and sides: Cut from focus fabric 4 strips measuring $4^{3}/_{4}$″x 40″. Cut from each strip 4 rectangles $4^{3}/_{4}$″x $10^{1}/_{2}$″, for a total of 16. Cut the remaining fabric into 6 equal-width strips ($2^{3}/_{4}$″) and set aside for border.
From the remaining 4 fabrics (2 lights and 2 darks), cut 2 strips measuring $5^{1}/_{2}$″x 40″ width of fabric. Cut 16 rectangles of each fabric measuring $3^{3}/_{8}$″x $5^{1}/_{2}$″.

Optional: Use the strip piece method: Create strip sets by cutting 2 strips each 5½"x 40" width of fabric. Pair a light strip with a dark and a light with a medium. Pin and sew these strip sets. You should have 2 sets. Press seam allowance to darker fabric. Cut from these sets units measuring 3⅜"x 10½". You will need 16 pairs. (Diagram 35)

Diagram 35

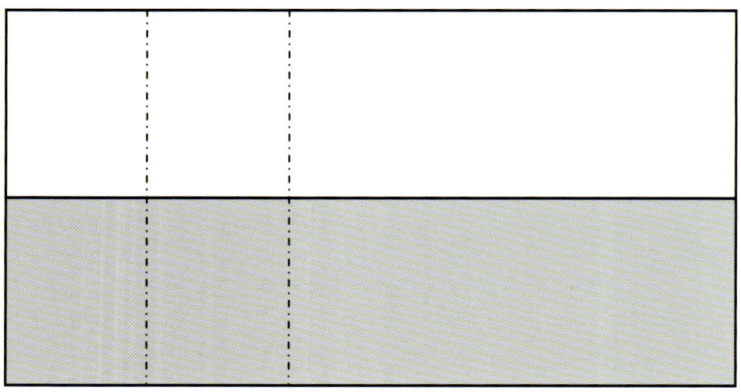

Border: Cut from the remaining light background fabric 6 strips 4″ wide and set aside for border. Cut 2 of these strips in half, creating 4 lengths of 22″, and set aside with border fabric.

Binding: Cut from binding fabric 6 strips measuring $22^{1}/_{2}$″x 40″and set aside.

Diagram 36

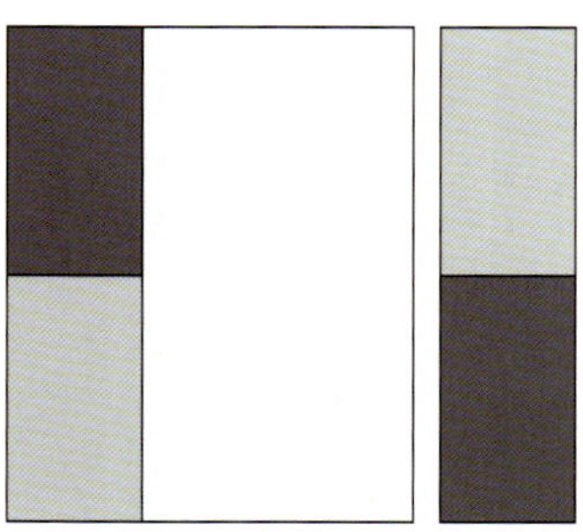

Block construction: Place side sets in two stacks. Sew one set on each side of the center piece, making sure that the light fabrics are in diagonal corners. Repeat process to complete 16 blocks. All the blocks will be the same. *(Diagram 36)*

Arrange the blocks on a work surface. Remember that the sides should have a pair of the same light color value in diagonal placement within the block. The quilt has 4 blocks across and 4 rows down. The blocks are placed in an alternating direction so that the same colors meet in the middle of 4 connecting blocks to give the appearance of a pinwheel.

Tip: It helps to think in terms of 4 in this quilt. All 4 sides are always in the same placement within the block.

Assembly: Sew together row 1 (blocks 1 and 2) and row 2 (blocks 1 and 2) to create the first unit. Sew together row 1 (blocks 3 and 4) and row 2 (blocks 3 and 4) to create the second unit. These two units are sewn together to complete the top half of the quilt top.

Sew together row 3 (blocks 1 and 2) and row 4 (blocks 1 and 2) to create unit 3.

The last unit consists of row 3 (blocks 3 and 4) and row 4 (block 3 and 4). These two units are sewn together to create the bottom half of the quilt top.

Sew the two halves together, aligning seams. Measure quilt top as in General Directions and make any necessary corrections.

Measure quilt top for borders: See General Instructions (see page 10).

Tip: Mark the quilt at middle and quarter points with a chalk marker. Mark the border strips at measurement points and use straight pins to align the border strips.

Inner border: Light fabric: join a full-length strip and a half strip with a 45-degree seam. See General Instructions on joining strips in the binding section. Repeat on all strips, making sure the seams are sewn in the same direction. Trim 2 strip sets to side length. Pin and sew one set to one side of quilt top, matching middle and quarter points. Trim the last two sets to the quilt width *plus* the width of the border strip. Pin and sew to top of quilt. Pin and sew last set to bottom of quilt. Press seams toward border.

Outer border: Join a full and a half strip into a set by sewing on a 45-degree angle, making sure all seams are sewn in the same direction. See General Instructions on joining binding strips. Repeat process to create 4 strip sets. Pin and sew one set to side of quilt. Pin and sew other set to opposite of quilt. Pin and sew a set to the top of the quilt, and trim even with the quilt top. Pin and sew the remaining set to the quilt bottom, trimming even with quilt. Press border seam allowances outward.

Baste the three layers—top, batting, and backing—and quilt as desired. This is an ideal pattern for a fancy quilting design.

Binding: See General Instructions.

Color Block

9 Color Block

50"x 50", 12" finished block, 5 blocks

This pattern is sure to please when made with bright, floral, or patriotic themed fabrics. The blocks are set on-point and joined with sashing and cornerstones. Quilt consists of 5 blocks; each block has 3 fabrics of the same color family. The blocks are framed with sashing and contrasting cornerstones at the intersections.

Fabric:

1 fat quarter .... contrasting color for cornerstones
3 fat quarters.................... in same color family per block
1/2 yard .... solid color for sashing
3/4 yard............................ background fabric for insets
1 yard .... border
1/2 yard .... binding if one color, or 3/8 yard each of four colors
3 yards............................. backing

Cutting: center $5^1/_2$"x $12^1/_2$", sides 4"x $6^1/_2$"

Centers and sides: Cut from each color group one strip for the center measuring $5^1/_2$"x $12^1/_2$". Set aside. From each of the remaining fabrics, cut one strip measuring 4"x $6^1/_2$".

Cornerstones: Cut from the cornerstone fabric 2 strips measuring $1^3/_4$"x 18". From these strips, cut 12 squares measuring $1^3/_4$" square.

Sashing: Cut from the sashing fabric 6 strips measuring $1^3/_4$"x 40". From these strips, cut 16 sections $12^1/_2$" long.

Background insets: Cut from background inset fabric one $20^1/_2$" square and two $11^1/_2$" squares. Cut the larger square in X-fashion to create 4 triangles. Cut the two smaller squares on the diagonal to create 4 half-square triangles.

Border: Cut 5 strips measuring 6"x 40".

Binding: Cut 6 strips measuring $2^1/_2$"x 40". If using a different color on each side, cut 2 strips from each color fabric.

Block construction: Pin two rectangles, 4"x $6^1/_2$", of the same color family together along the 4" edge. *(Diagram 37)*

Diagram 37

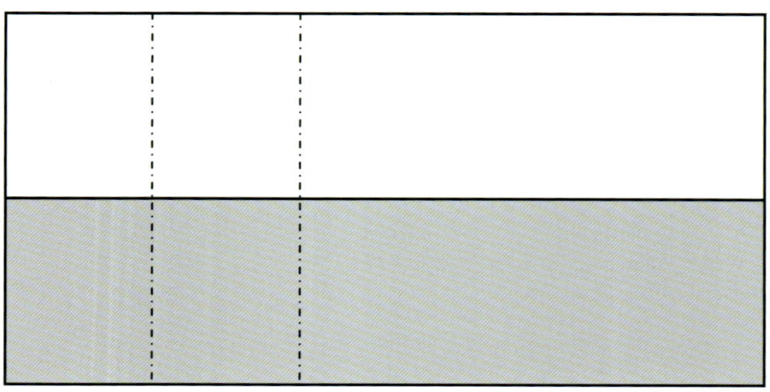

Sew one set to each side of the center, making sure that the light colors are in diagonal corners. Repeat process to complete 1 block of each color. Press seam allowances to the center. *(Diagram 38)*

Diagram 38

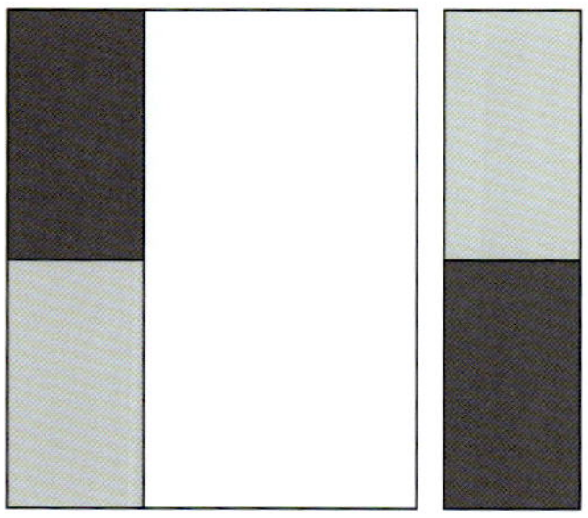

Assembly: Place blocks on-point on a design surface. Look at the rows diagonally rather than horizontally. Refer to picture often.

Row 1: one block in upper left position.

Row 2: three blocks across the middle.

Row 3: one block in lower right position.

Pin a sashing strip on the left side of each block. Pin a sashing strip to the right side of the end of row blocks. Sew row 2 blocks with sashing to make a completed row. *(Diagram 39)*

Diagram 39

Cornerstones and sashing: Sew a cornerstone to each end of a sashing strip. Sew this strip to the top of the upper left block, matching seam intersections. Sew a cornerstone to a sashing until you have 4 cornerstones and 3 sashing pieces in a continuous strip. Repeat to create a second strip. Sew one strip to the top of the three-block row, matching seam intersections. Refer to picture. *(Diagram 40)*

Diagram 40

Sew the second strip to the bottom of the same continuous block row. Sew a cornerstone to each end of a sashing strip. Sew this strip to the bottom of the lower right block, matching seam intersections. Press seam allowance to the cornerstone.

Insets: Sew a quarter-cut (X) triangle to the left side of the row 1 block. Pin and sew a quarter-cut triangle to the right side of the row 1 block. The straight edge is facing down. *(Diagram 41)*

Diagram 41

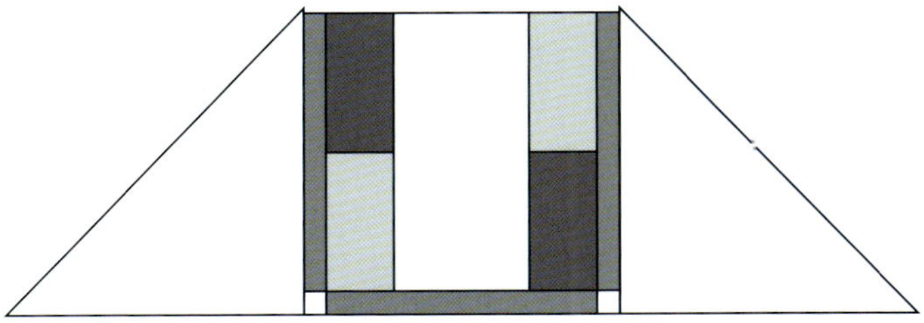

Row 2: Do not sew a triangle to this row. Row 2 will have corner triangles on both ends.

Row 3: Sew an X-cut triangle to the left side of the row 3 block. Sew an X-cut triangle to the right side of the row 3 block.

The direction should be opposite of the row 1. If row 1 is like the diagram, flip the diagram to look opposite with the straight edge facing up.

Sew row 1 to row 2, matching seam intersections. Sew rows 1 and 2 to row 3, making sure the seam intersections match. Press seam allowances to the sashing.

Diagram 42

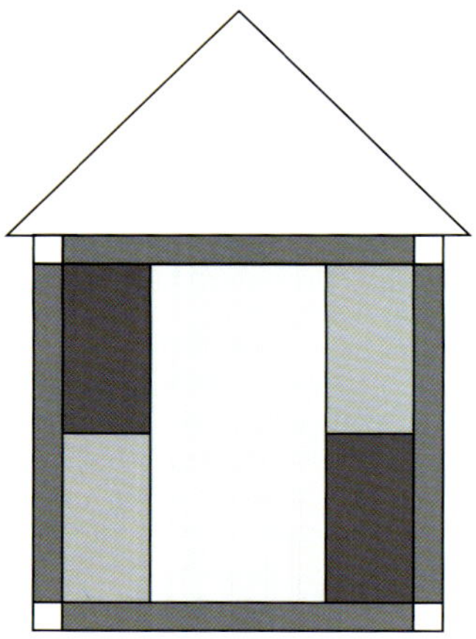

Corners: Pin and sew a half-square triangle with the long edge (diagonal) along the sashing top of the corner block. Repeat on remaining three corners. Press seam allowance outward. *(Diagrams 42&43)*

Diagram 43

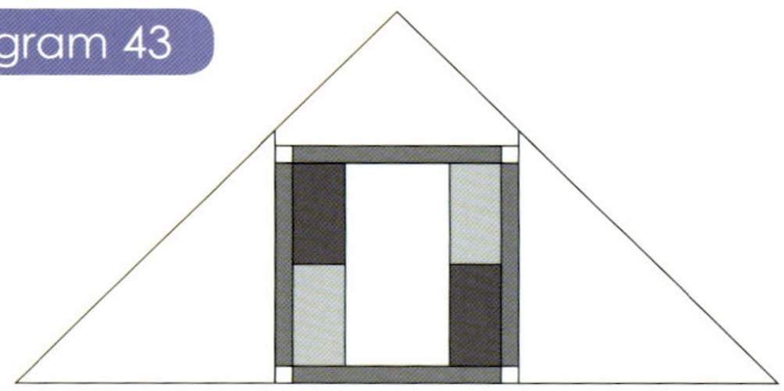

Measure quilt top for borders: See General Instructions (see page 10). Trim the excess along the outside for a straight edge. I opted to trim half of the outside cornerstones. Remember to leave a 1/4″ seam allowance if trimming to the cornerstone.

Tip: Mark the quilt at middle and quarter points with a chalk marker. Mark the border strips at measurement points and use straight pins to align the border strips.

Border: Check measurements. One strip should be long enough for a side of the quilt top. Sew a strip to each side of the quilt top. Sew two lengths together to create a strip for the top edge of the quilt and trim excess. Sew remaining excess length to last strip for bottom of quilt. Press seam allowances to the border.
Baste the three layers—top, batting, and backing—and quilt as desired. This is an ideal pattern for a fancy quilting design.

Binding: See General Instructions.

Rose Garden. 67"x 67", 10" finished block. The layout is horizontal in alternating directions. Made by Carolyn Perry Goins, 2007.

Close-up of *Rose Garden* block

A

C

B

D

A) Zombie Comfort. 72"x 72", 15" finished block. The layout is horizontal in alternating directions. Made by Renelda Peldunas-Harter, 2014. No pattern given for this size block.

B) Close-up of *Zombie Comfort* block.

C) Abby Road. 62"x 62", 8" finished block. The layout is on the diagonal without borders. Made by Nancine Pike of Cottage Chintz Long Arm Quilting Services, 2014.

D) Blue Bubbles. 42"x 42", 6" finished block. The layout is horizontal in alternating directions. Made by Renelda Peldunas-Harter, 2014.

Blissful Flowers. 46"x 46", 12" finished block. The layout is horizontal in alternating directions. Made by Carolyn Perry Goins, 2010.

Close up of *Blissful Flowers* block.

Grandpa's Ties

11

Grandpa's Ties

51"x 69", 12" finished block, 8 blocks, on-point

This is a long lap quilt. I made this for my husband, who is 6′ 3″. It takes a long quilt to cover his legs when he is in the recliner. This pattern features one set of side rectangles with the same color as the center strip, but in a different fabric. The opposing side rectangles are background-value fabric (it need not be the same fabric as the triangular insets). It is set on the diagonal—2 blocks across, 3 blocks down, and 2 blocks in the center. The blocks are framed with sashing and cornerstones.

Fabric: *Background requirement includes the block sides, insets, and corners.*

$^1/_2$ yard .... blue center
$^1/_2$ yard .... blue sides
$^1/_2$ yard .... red center
$^1/_2$ yard .... red sides
$^5/_8$ yard .... sides if different than background fabric
$^1/_2$ yard .... sashing
2 yards............................. background
1 fat quarter or $^1/_4$ yard ..... cornerstones
$^5/_8$ yard .... inner border
1 yard .... outer border
$^1/_2$ yard .... binding
$3^1/_4$ yards .... backing

Cutting: Strips are cut width of fabric. Four blocks of each color fabric will be the same.

Centers and sides: Cut 4 center strips of each color measuring 5 1/2"x 12 1/2". From the side color fabric, cut 2 sides measuring 4"x 6 1/2".

Background sides: Cut 3 strips 4"x 40". From the strips, cut rectangles measuring 4"x 6 1/2". You will need 16 rectangles.

Sashing strips: Cut 8 strips measuring 2"x 40". Cut 24 sashing strips measuring 2"x 12 1/2".

Cornerstones: From the cornerstone fabric, cut 1 strip 2"x 40". You will need 17 cornerstones measuring 2"x 2" .

Background: Cut two squares measuring 20 1/4". Cut in X-fashion, creating 8 inset triangles. Only 6 will be used. From the background fabric, cut 2 squares measuring 11 1/2" inches. Cut on the diagonal to create a total of 4 half-square triangles for the corners.

Inner border: Cut 6 strips 1 1/2"x 40".

Outer border: Cut 6 strips 4 1/2"x 40".

Diagram 44

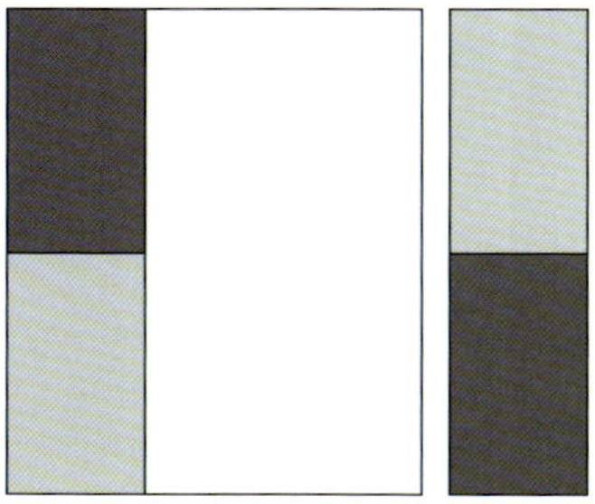

Block construction: See General Construction (see page 10). Make sure the color placement of the sides is in the same position in each block. *(Diagram 44)*

Press the seam allowances to the center strip. Place finished blocks on-point on work surface in the order desired: 2 blocks across and 3 blocks down. We will add the background triangles later.

Sashing: Sew a sashing strip to the left and right sides of each block. Sew a cornerstone to one end of each strip. Sew a cornerstone strip to another sashing strip. Sew strip to the top of block. Repeat on remaining strips. Place blocks back onto work surface as steps are completed. Place blocks into rows according to the diagonal layout and sew.

Diagram 45

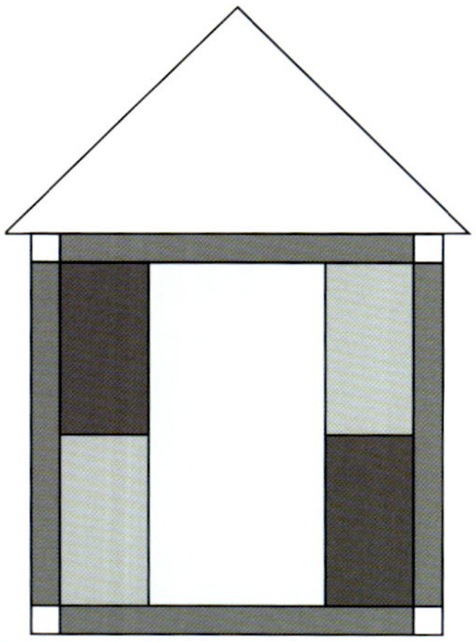

Row 1: 1 block; row 2: 3 blocks; row 3: 3 blocks; row 4: 1 block. Sew a background corner triangle to the top of the upper left block. Sew an inset triangle on each side of the upper left block with straight edges along the top. *(Diagrams 45&46)*

Diagram 46

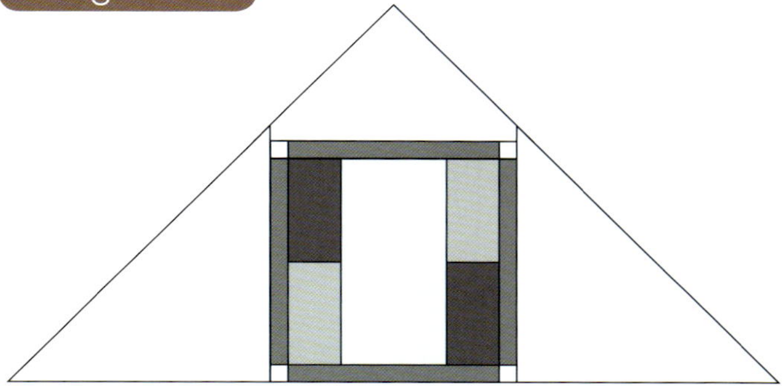

Row 2 has three blocks. Sew an inset triangle to the left of row 2. Sew a corner triangle to the right side of the third block.

Row 3 has three blocks. Sew a corner block to the left side of the lower left block. Sew an inset block to the right side of the third block. *(Diagram 47)*

Diagram 47

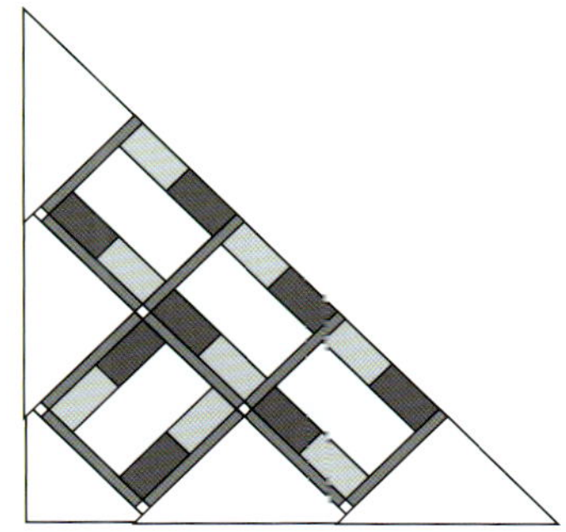

Row 4: Sew a corner triangle to the top of the lower right block. Sew an inset triangle to each side of this block. Sew rows 1 and 2 with right sides together, making sure the seam intersections meet. Sew rows 3 and 4 with right sides together, aligning seams. Sew the two sections together, aligning seams. Press the seam allowances to the sashing. Square up and trim.

Measure quilt top for borders: See General Instructions.

Tip: *Mark the quilt at middle and quarter points with a chalk marker. Mark the border strips at measurement points and use straight pins to align the border strips.*

Inner border: Sew two strips together with an angle seam to create one long strip (see General Instructions). Repeat for a second long strip. Sew one long set to each side of the quilt and trim ends. Sew remaining strips to top and bottom edges of quilt and trim.

Outer border: Repeat steps for inner border.

Baste the three layers—top, batting, and backing—and quilt as desired.

Binding: See General Instructions.

Baby Fiona Chevrons

12

Baby Fiona Chevrons

35"x 40", 8" finished block, 30 blocks, on-point

This baby quilt features the modern trend of chevrons across the surface. Bright colors will keep the baby's attention. Here the Fiona block has been modified; the side rectangle is the same length as the center strip. The center strip contains the background fabric and the sides are the focus colors. This pattern requires exact color placements and numbers of color blocks.

Fabric:

1 yard .... background
1/2 yard .... each of 4 fabric colors
1/3 yard .... binding color of choice
1 1/4 yard........................ .. backing fabric

Cutting: center 4″x 8$^1/_2$″, **sides** 2$^3/_4$″x 8$^1/_2$″
Strips are cut width of fabric. Quilt requires 6 blocks of blue and purple, 6 blocks of green and purple, 8 blocks of blue and orange, and 10 blocks of green and orange, for a total of 30 blocks.

Centers and sides: Cut from background fabric 3 strips measuring 8$^1/_2$″x 40″ for center. Cut from each strip 10 lengths measuring 4″x 8$^1/_2$″.
Cut from each color fabric 2 strips measuring 8$^1/_2$″x 40″. There will be leftover fabric from each strip. Orange fabric may need 3 strips.
Cut from purple strips 12 lengths measuring 2$^3/_4$″x 8$^1/_2$″. There will be leftover fabric.
Cut from blue strips 14 lengths measuring 2$^3/_4$″x 8$^1/_2$″.
Cut from green strips 16 lengths measuring 2$^3/_4$″x 8$^1/_2$″.
Cut from orange strips 18 lengths measuring 2$^3/_4$″x 8$^1/_2$″.

Binding: Cut from the binding fabric 4 strips measuring 2$^1/_2$″x 40″. Set aside.

Block construction: Piece the blocks to the center background fabric in the color order described above. Some of these blocks will be used for side insets. Press seam allowance to color side. *(Diagram 48)*

Diagram 48

Layout: Diagonal layout; the blocks are laid on-point. Place blocks on work surface in color order as shown. Each block will be "pointing" in an alternating direction (one block left, next block right) to create the zigzag effect. Each connecting block will match a rectangle in the previous block to create the zigzag effect. The inset block will be added later.

Row 1: 1 block—green and purple

Row 2: 3 blocks—blue and orange, blue and purple, green and purple

Row 3: 5 blocks—green and purple, green and orange, blue and orange, blue and purple, green and purple

Row 4: 5 blocks—blue and orange, blue and purple, green and purple, orange and green, blue and orange

Row 5: 3 blocks—blue and orange, purple and blue, green and purple

Row 6: 1 block—blue and orange

Assembly: Sew blocks together, creating diagonal rows. Place completed rows back in place on work surface. Place a color-coordinating block at the side of an end block and mark a line 1″ beyond where the block comes to a point. This will be a 45-degree line marking the side edge of the quilt. Trim the excess inset block on the mark line.

Tip: Be generous with the marked line. It is better to trim again later than to be short of fabric.

The trimmed edges will be bias, so handle carefully. The excess of the block may be used on another row as needed, making sure color lines match. Press seam allowances to the right on even-numbered rows, to the left on odd-numbered rows. *(Diagram 49)*

Diagram 49

Pin and sew the rows together. The straight edge of the setting triangles will butt up against the block in the next row.

Note the change of direction for setting the triangle in rows 4 and 5. (Diagram 50)

Diagram 50

Each top corner will have a trimmed bias block at the top. Refer to picture for placement of the block direction. The edges will be bias; basting by hand or machine (long stitch) will prevent stretching.

Press row seam allowances in direction of choice. Baste the top, batting, and backing fabric. Quilt as desired. I chose to stitch in the ditch of the color lengths. I machine stitched a free-hand style of hairpin loops across the background areas. Trim square as needed.

Binding: See general instructions.

Full Bloom

13 Full Bloom

67"x 67", 12" finished block, 13 blocks, on-point

Twelve of *Full Bloom's* 13 blocks have three different floral fabrics and one background fabric. The 13th block features flowers cut from the floral fabrics and arranged in a circular design on the background fabric. The setting insets use the same background fabric. The blocks are set on-point and joined with sashing and cornerstones. Use your favorite floral print for the border.

Fabric:

3 fat quarters	or 12 floral scraps, minimum 6″x 13″ per block.
1/4 yard	or 1 fat quarter for cornerstones
5/8 yard	sashing
2 yards	border
5/8 yard	binding, if not using leftover of border fabric
4 yards	backing at 40″ wide
1/8 yard	or scrap of green for appliqué leaves
2 yards	background fabric

Cutting: **center** 5 1/2" x 12 1/2", **sides** 4" x 6 1/2"

Centers and sides: Cut from each floral/focus fabric one 5 1/2" x 12 1/2". Cut one 4" x 6 1/2" side rectangle from each floral coordinated fabric.

Background: Cut two 4" x 40" strips from the solid fabric. Cut from the two strips a total of 24 rectangles measuring 4" x 6 1/2". Cut one square measuring 14" square for the center appliqué.

Sashing: Cut 2 sashing strips measuring 12 1/2" x 40" (length of fabric). From these, cut 36 strips measuring 1 3/4" x 12 1/2" (length of fabric). Each strip will yield 20; you will need 36.

Cornerstones: Cut 3 1 3/4" x 18" strips from the cornerstone fabric (fat quarter). From these strips, cut 24 squares measuring 1 3/4" square.

Setting triangles: Cut from the background fabric 2 large squares measuring 20 1/4" square. Cut the square diagonally in X-fashion. Repeat on the second square. You will have 8 triangles. Set aside.
From the background fabric, cut 2 11 1/2" squares. Cut each square once on the diagonal, creating 2 triangles. Repeat on second 11 1/2" square. You now have 4 triangles to be used as corners. Set aside.

Border: Cut 4 strips length (straight grain) of fabric measuring 7" x 72". The remaining fabric may be used for binding.
Optional: border width may be increased to 8" without sacrificing leftovers for binding.

Binding: Cut 4 strips length of fabric from border fabric measuring 2 1/2" x 72". If using a different fabric, cut 8 strips measuring 2 1/2" x 40" width of fabric.

Block construction: See General Instructions (see page 10). The focus fabric will be the center. Each side will have 1 floral and 1 background sewn together. The floral print will be different on each side and placed diagonally when the strip is sewn to the center. Press seam allowance to center. Complete 12 blocks in this fashion. *(Diagram 51)*

Diagram 51

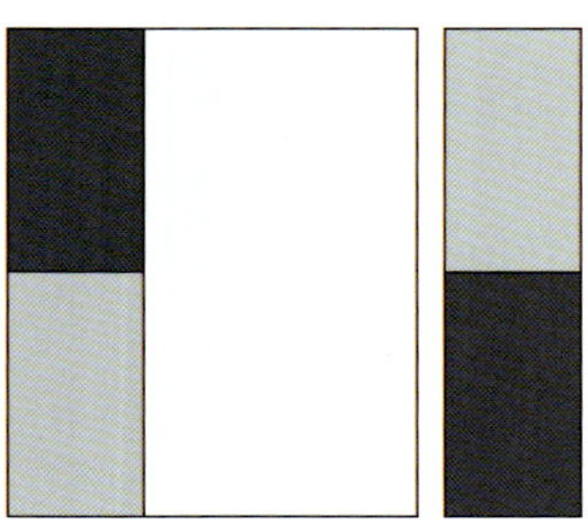

Appliqué: Fold the 14" square into fourths and lightly press. Place a light pencil mark at each fold line 4" from the center of the square. These will be guidelines for the appliqué wreath. Cut flowers from the remaining collection of floral fabric. Arrange in a circular design. Add leaves by cutting a 2" strip (width of fabric) from scrap in random shapes, or trace the pattern provided. Baste with needle and thread or fuse in place when appliqué is completed. Trim the block to a 12 1/2" square. To appliqué the block, you may use traditional needle turn, the raw edge method, or the fusible method.

Assembly: Arrange blocks on-point on work surface in desired order. Refer to the picture for block direction. The appliqué block will be placed in the middle. Think of the rows as diagonal rather than horizontal.
Sew a sashing strip on the left side of each block. Sew an additional sashing strip to right side of the last block in each row.

Cornerstones and sashing: Sew a cornerstone to each end of a sashing strip.

Row 1: Sew this strip to the top of row 1 (upper left, single block), aligning seam intersections.

Row 2: Sew 4 cornerstones and 3 sashing pieces in a continuous strip. Sew to the top of row 2, aligning the seams. *(Diagram 52)*

Diagram 52

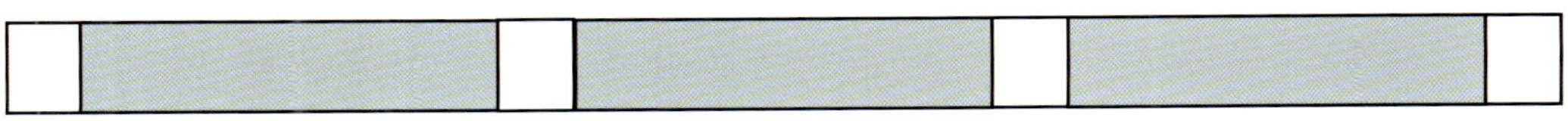

Row 3: Sew a cornerstone to the sashing to create 6 cornerstones and 5 sashing strips. Sew to the top of row 3, aligning the seams.

Row 4: Sew together 6 cornerstones and 5 sashing strips. Pin and sew to the top of row 4, aligning the seams.

Note: This row has the same number of cornerstones and sashing as row 3.

Row 5: Sew together 4 cornerstones and 3 sashing strips. Sew to the top of row 5, aligning seams.

Row 6: Sew together 2 cornerstones and 1 sashing strip. Sew to the top of row 6, aligning the seams.

Setting triangles: Row 1: Pin a triangle to each side of the sashing so that the straight edge is facing down, and sew. *(Diagram 53)*

Diagram 53

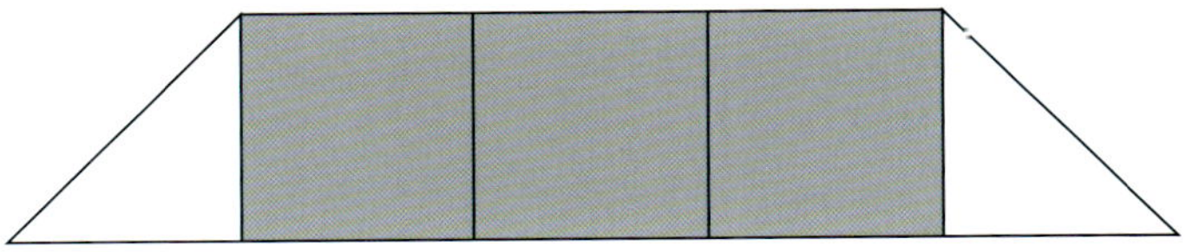

Row 2: Sew a setting triangle to the sashing (left side) of the first block in the row so that the straight edge is facing down. Sew a setting triangle to the sashing (right side) of the last block in the row so that the straight edge is facing down.

Row 3: Do *not* sew triangles to this row.

Diagram 54

Row 4: Sew a setting triangle in a new direction. The straight edge of the triangles should now face up. *(Diagram 54)*

Row 5: Sew a setting triangle to the sashing (left side) of the first block and to the last block sashing (right side) with straight edge facing up.

Press seam allowances of even-number rows to the right and odd-number rows to the left.

Sew rows together. The straight edge of the setting triangles will butt up against the block in the next row.

Note the change of direction for setting triangles in rows 4 and 5. Sewing will be easier if rows are sewn into pairs, then sewn to the next set of pairs. The weight of the top will be distributed, making it easier to handle.

Tip: Mark the quilt at middle and quarter points with a chalk marker. Mark the border strips at measurement points and use straight pins to align the border strips.

Sew a triangle with the long edge against the sashing top of the corner blocks. Press the row seams in one direction.

Measure quilt top for borders: See General Instructions. Trim excess fabric at the edges, leaving straight 1/4″ seam allowance along all side edges.

Borders: Sew a border strip to each side of the quilt and trim excess. Repeat with top and bottom strips. Press seam allowances to border.

Baste the three layers together and quilt. This quilt features a meandering vine.

Binding: See General Instructions.

Diagram 55

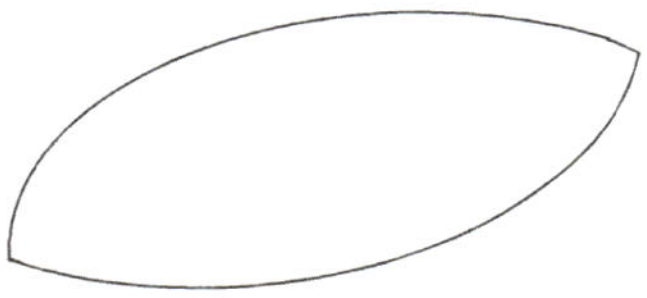

Leaf tracing is for the center block appliqué. Remember that leaves are not perfectly shaped. Be creative. The tracing is approximately 2″ long. Add 1/4″ seam allowance. *(Diagram 55)*

14 Double Trouble

69"x 69" 4", 8" finished blocks, 32 large blocks and 64 small blocks

This quilt is a result of waking in the middle of the night and thinking...what if I use two block sizes in one quilt? The name Double Trouble refers to the two sizes of blocks used, not the difficulty level. The trick is to use a small block that is half the size of the larger block. Four small blocks are sewn in 4-patch fashion to create a block equal to the larger block. This creates a pinwheel effect and offers many layout possibilities.

The quilt shown uses a 4″ small block and 8″ large block to make a 69″x 69″ quilt. To make a 97″x 97″ quilt, use a 6″ small block and 12″ large block. If you do not want a square quilt, make it rectangular. Just remember to adjust the number of blocks and yardage.

Fabric:

3 yards............................ focus fabrics to be used for centers, outer border, and binding
1/2 yard each .... large block sides, 4 colors that complement the focus fabric
5/8 yard each .... small block sides, 2 colors that complement the focus fabric
3/8 yard .... inner border, same fabric as a small side
1/2 yard .... binding, if different from the focus fabric
4 1/2 yards........................ backing, if using 40″-wide fabric

Double Trouble

Cutting:

Finished size 69″x 69″

BLOCK SIZE	CENTER	SIDES
4″	2½″x 4½″	1½″x 2½″
8″	4″x 8½″	2¾″x 4½″

Finished size 97″x 97″

BLOCK SIZE	CENTER	SIDES
6″	3″x 6½″	2¼″x 3½″
12″	5½″x 12½″	4″x 6½″

Side color fabrics will always be in the same position; do not vary color placements.

Centers and sides: Large block: On the focus fabric, cutting the centers and binding first allows the remaining fabric to be divided into wider borders if desired. A wider border would require 7 strips. Cut 4 focus fabric strips measuring 8½″x 40″. From these strips, cut 10 rectangles each measuring 4″x 8½″. Cut 2 more rectangles from the remaining strip. You will need a total of 32.

From each of 4 side fabrics, cut 3 strips measuring 4½″x 40″. From two of the color strips, cut 14 rectangles measuring 2¾″ x 4½″. Cut 4 more rectangles from the remaining strips. You will need 32 of each color.

Optional: Use a strip piecing method by sewing two different-color strips together lengthwise. Press seam allowance to darker fabric. Cut segments measuring 2¾"x 8½", yielding 14 sets per strip. Repeat with the strips of the same color. (Diagram 60)

Diagram 60

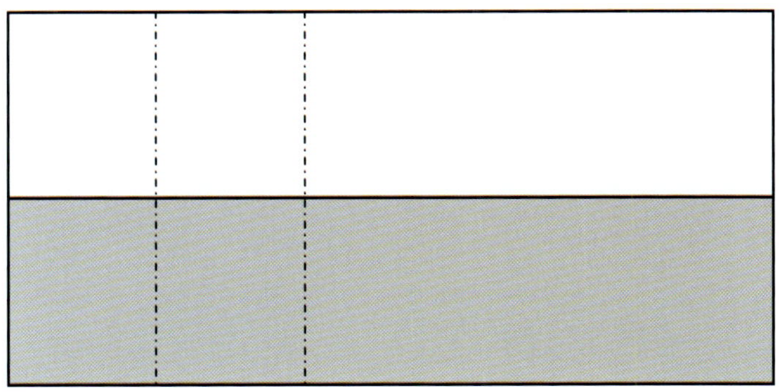

Sew the other two color strips together lengthwise. Press seam allowance to darker fabric. Cut sets measuring 2¾″x 8½″, yielding 14 sets per strip. Repeat with the strips of the same color. You will need 32 of each color set.

Small block. From the focus fabric, cut 4 strips measuring 4½″x 40″. From the strips, cut rectangles measuring 2½″x 4½″. You will need 64.

Optional: To use the strip piecing method, cut from side fabrics 5 strips of each color measuring 2½"x 40". Pin and sew one of each color together along the length of strip. Repeat on all strips. Each strip should yield 10 sets. Press seam allowance to darker fabric. Cut from each strip sets measuring 1½"x 4½". You will need a total of 64 of each color set.

Inner border: Cut 6 strips of chosen inner border fabric measuring 1½″x 40″.
Outer border: Cut 6 strips of focus fabric measuring 6″x 40″.

Tip: Cutting the centers and binding first allows the remaining fabric to be divided into wider borders if desired. A wider border would require 7 strips.

Binding: Cut 7 strips of focus or chosen fabric measuring 2½″x 40″. Set aside.

Diagram 61

Block construction:

Large block. Pin and sew side rectangles in consistent order and position. If using the strip piecing method, side sections have already been sewn. Sew side set to center in a consistent position. Sew second color set to opposite side of center to equal 32 blocks. Press seam allowances to the center. *(Diagram 61)*

Small block: Pin and sew rectangles in consistent order and position. If using strip piecing method, side sections have already been sewn. Sew side set to center in a consistent position. Sew second color set to opposite side of center to equal 64 blocks. Press seam allowance to center.

Place 4 small blocks on work surface to form a square. Each center strip should point in a different direction. Sew blocks and place back into position on the work surface. Sew two sets of blocks together, matching the seam allowances. Continue to sew 4 blocks together in this manner to create 32 blocks equal in size to the larger block. *(Diagram 62)*

Diagram 62

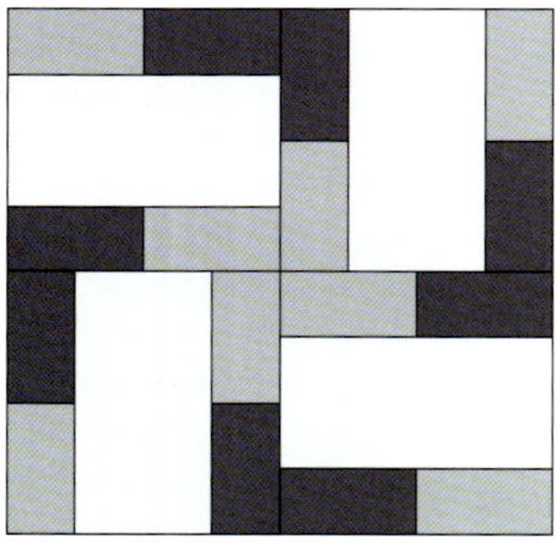

Assembly: Refer to the picture for proper block placement. The large blocks have been turned so that the colors stair step to create a diamond shape. The lower half of the quilt top stair-steps in an opposite color.

Place all blocks on a work surface and keep them there throughout the sewing process. The word "small" will refer to the 4 small blocks units. The diagram shows directional placement of the large blocks. *(Diagram 63)*

Diagram 63

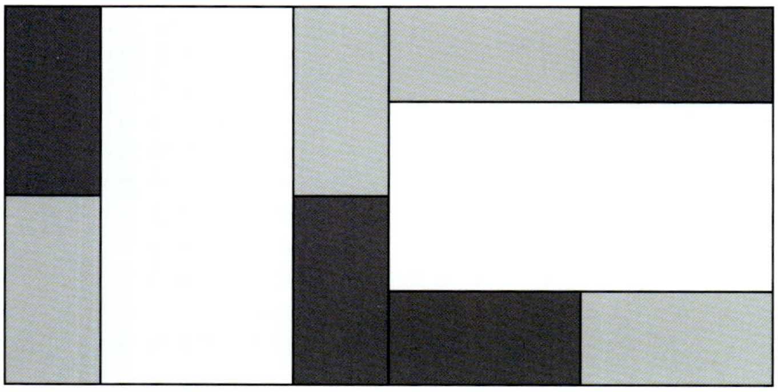

Row 1: large vertical, small, large vertical, large horizontal, large vertical, small, large vertical.

Row 2: small, large vertical, large horizontal, small, large horizontal, large vertical, small.

Row 3: large vertical, large horizontal, small, large horizontal, small, large horizontal, large vertical.

Row 4: large horizontal, small, large vertical, large vertical large vertical, small, large horizontal.

Row 5: large vertical, large horizontal, small, large horizontal, small, large horizontal, large vertical.

Row 6: small, large vertical, large horizontal, small, large horizontal, large vertical, small.

Row 7: large vertical, small, large vertical, large horizontal, large vertical, small, large vertical.

For each row pin and sew blocks together and replace on work surface in proper position. Repeat process to complete all rows. Press seam allowances of odd-numbered rows to the left and even-numbered rows to the right.

Sew rows 1 and 2 together, matching seam intersections.
Sew rows 3 and 4 together, matching seam intersections.
Sew rows 1 and 2 to rows 3 and 4, matching seam intersections.
Sew rows 5 and 6 together, matching seam intersections.
Sew rows 5 and 6 to row 7, matching seam intersections.
Sew top half (rows 1, 2, 3, and 4) to bottom half (rows 5, 6, and 7), matching seam intersections.
Press seam allowances in one direction.

Measure quilt top for borders: See General Instructions (see page 10).

> **Tip:** *Mark the quilt at middle and quarter points with a chalk marker. Mark the border strips at measurement points and use straight pins to align the border strips.*

Inner border: See General Instructions on binding. Sew 2 strips together with angle seams. Repeat on second set of strips. Trim to length. *The trimmed leftover strip should be long enough to be joined to the next strip.*
Sew one trimmed strip to each side of the quilt. Repeat on top and bottom, trimming excess. Re-measure the length and sides for the next border plus 1″.

Outer border: Repeat instructions for inner border. Press seam allowances to the outside. Baste the top, batting, and backing, and quilt as desired. An edge to edge, all-over design works well.

Binding: See General Instructions.

Christmas Wrappings

15

Christmas Wrappings

42"x 76", 12" finished block, 10 blocks, on-point

This holiday quilt reminds me of crumpled wrapping paper on the floor after the gifts have been opened. The fabric in the blocks are scraps, making this design ideal for thinning the fabric stash. The background fabric is consistent throughout and provides a place for the eye to rest.

This quilt is constructed much like Grandpa's Ties. Both quilts are set on-point and are long. The light and dark colors may be placed randomly, like paper on the floor.

Fabric:

This quilt will fit a standard-width backing fabric.

1 1/2 yards........................ background for border and insets
1/4" yard.......................... each 6 or more darks and mediums
3/4 yard........................... equal to of one or more lights
3/4 yard........................... bright for inner border and binding
2 1/4 yard......................... backing (44" x 81")

Cutting: **center** 5½″x 12½″, **sides** 4″x 6½″

Directions are given as if scraps are used, rather than continuous yardage.

Centers and sides: Darks and mediums: From various fabrics, cut 10 centers measuring 5½″x 12½″. Cut 4 sides measuring 4″x 6½″ from each fabric. Lights: Cut 40 sides measuring 4″x 6½″.

Inner border: Cut 6 strips width of fabric measuring 1½″x 40″. Cut remaining fabric into 6 strips 2½″x 40″ and set aside for binding. Join 2 sets of 2. See binding section in General Directions for this technique.

Outer border and insets: Cut from background fabric 6 strips width of fabric measuring 4″x 40″ for outer borders. Join 2 strips together and repeat for a second pair. Cut 2 squares measuring 18½″ and cut each square once on the diagonal to equal 4 corner triangles. Cut 1 square measuring 18½″ and cut in X-fashion for insets.

Diagram 56

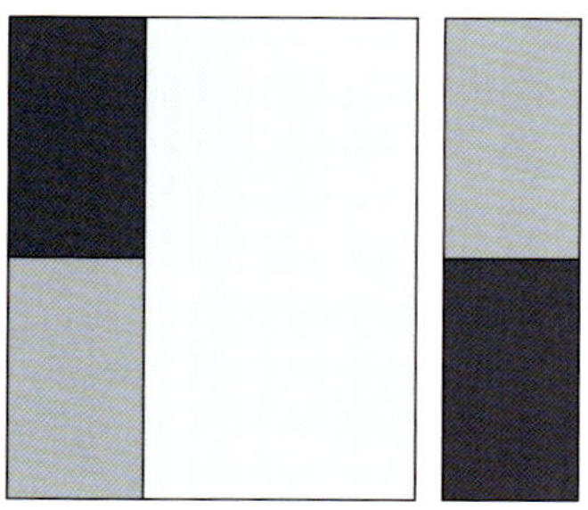

Block construction: Piece blocks according to General Instructions (see page 10). Each center is a dark fabric; the sides will have one light and a medium or dark for contrast. *(Diagram 56)*

Assembly: Arrange completed blocks on a work surface. Place corner and inset triangles on work surface in appropriate position.

Row 1: Sew two upper left blocks together. Press seam allowance to left. Sew the upper left corner triangle to the edge of row 1. Sew an inset triangle to the lower left of row 1. *(Diagram 57)*

Diagram 57

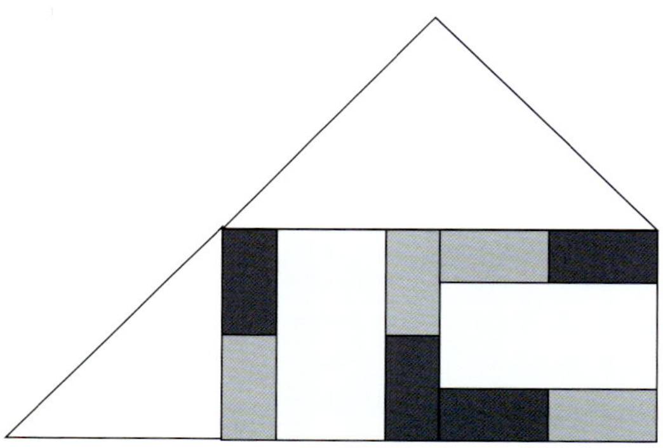

Row 2: Sew the next 3 blocks together to create row 2. Press seam allowance to the right. Sew an inset triangle to the lower left of row 2. *(Diagram 58)*

Diagram 58

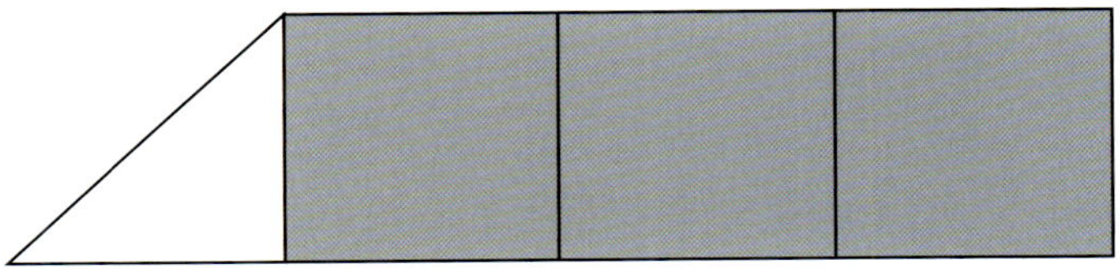

Sew rows 1 and 2 together, matching seam intersections. The top right blocks should be even. Sew a corner triangle to the upper right corner.

Row 3: Sew the next 3 blocks together. Press seam allowance to the left. Sew an inset to the side of the last block. *(Diagram 59)*

Diagram 59

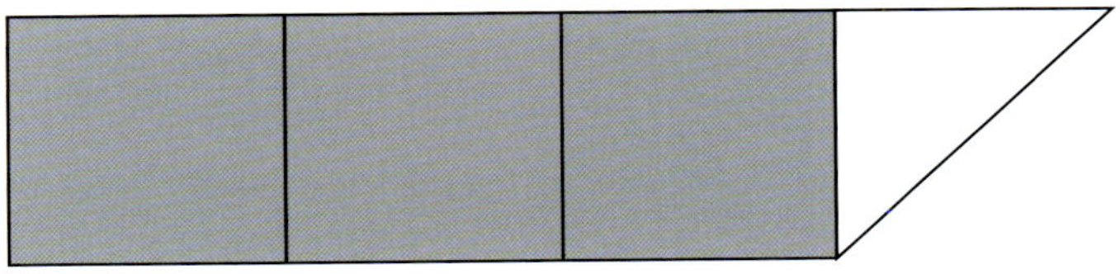

Row 4: Sew last two blocks together. Press seam allowance to the right. Sew an inset triangle to upper side of block in row 4. Sew rows 3 and 4, matching seam intersections. Sew a corner triangle to the lower left and lower right corners. Press seam allowances in one direction and trim edges even.

Measure quilt top for borders: See General Instructions.

Tip: Mark the quilt at middle and quarter points with chalk and straight pins to match the border strips. Also mark the border strips at measurement points.

Inner border: Join 2 strips together following General Instructions on binding. Repeat for a second set. Trim 2 sets to the length measurement (top to bottom) plus 1". Sew one set to each side of the quilt and trim. Repeat on top and bottom edges. Press seam allowances to the border.

Outer border: Follow General Instructions for binding and repeat as above. Press border seam allowances outward.

Baste the top, batting, and backing, and quilt as desired. I quilted meandering holly leaves across the surface.

Binding: See General Instructions.

Quilt Credits

Abby Road. Made and quilted by Nancine Pike of Cottage Chintz Long Arm Quilting Services, Virginia, 2014

Baby Fiona. Chevrons made and quilted by Carolyn Perry Goins, fabric donated by Windham Fabrics, Virginia, 2014

Blissful Flowers. Made and quilted by Carolyn Perry Goins, Virginia, 2010

Blue Bubbles. Made and quilted by Renelda Peldunas-Harter, Virginia, 2014

Building Blocks. Made and quilted by Carolyn Perry Goins, fabrics donated by Windham Fabric, Virginia, 2014

Caribbean. Made by Renelda Peldunas-Harter, quilted by Carolyn Perry Goins, fabric donated by Hoffman Fabrics of California, Virginia, 2010

Christmas Wrappings. Made and quilted by Carolyn Perry Goins, Virginia, 2014

Cinnamon & Spice. Made and quilted by Carolyn Perry Goins, Virginia, 2014

Color Block. Made by Carolyn Perry Goins, quilted by Christy Dillon of My Creative Stitches, Virginia, 2006

Coral Sea. Made by Carolyn Perry Goins, quilted by Renelda Peldunas-Harter, Virginia, 2011

Double Trouble. Made and quilted by Carolyn Perry Goins, Virginia, 2014

Full Bloom. Made and quilted by Carolyn Perry Goins, Virginia, 2007

Grandpa's Ties. Made and quilted by Carolyn Perry Goins, Virginia, 2009

Red Poppies. Made and quilted by Carolyn Perry Goins, Virginia, 2013

Rose Garden. Made and quilted by Carolyn Perry Goins, 2008, Virginia

Tea Time. Made and quilted by Carolyn Perry Goins, Virginia, 2009

Texas Two-Step. Made and quilted by Carolyn Perry Goins, Virginia, 2009

Woven Rust. Made by Carolyn Perry Goins and Renelda Peldunas-Harter, quilted by Carolyn Perry Goins, Virginia, 2009

Zombie Comfort. Made by Renelda Peldunas-Harter, quilted by Carolyn Perry Goins, Virginia, 2014

Resources

Anderson, Alex. *Shopping with Alex Anderson* (Concord, Calif: C & T Publishing, 2000); www.ctpublishing.com.

Aurifil Threads™, 184 Shuman Blvd. Suite 200, Naperville, Ill. 60563; www.aurifill.com.

Brown, Lynn Roddy. *Simple Strategies for Scrap Quilts* (Bothell, Wash.: Martingale Publishing, 2006).

Dillon, Christy. My Creative Stitches, Boyce, Virginia;

www.mycreativestitches.net.

CPG Designs L.L.C., *Patterns with the Beginner in Mind*, Hamilton, Virginia; www.cpgquiltdesigns.com.

Hoffman Fabrics of California, 25792 Obrero Drive, Mission Viejo, California; www.hoffmanfabrics.com

Peldunas-Harter, Renelda, USA Ret. *From Ensign's Bars to Colonel's Stars* (Atglen, Pa.: Schiffer Publishing, 2014).

Pike, Nancine, Cottage Chintz Long Arm Quilting Services, Round Hill, Virginia; www.cottagechintz.com.

Webb Fabrics, 116 N. Bailey, Purcellville, Virginia 20132; www.webfabrics.net.

Windham Fabrics/Braum Textile Mills, 812 Jersey Ave., Jersey City, NJ 07310; www.windhamfabrics.com.

Wonderfil Threads™, Bay 3, 2915 19th St. NE, Calgary, AB T2E 7A2 Canada; www.wonderfil.net.